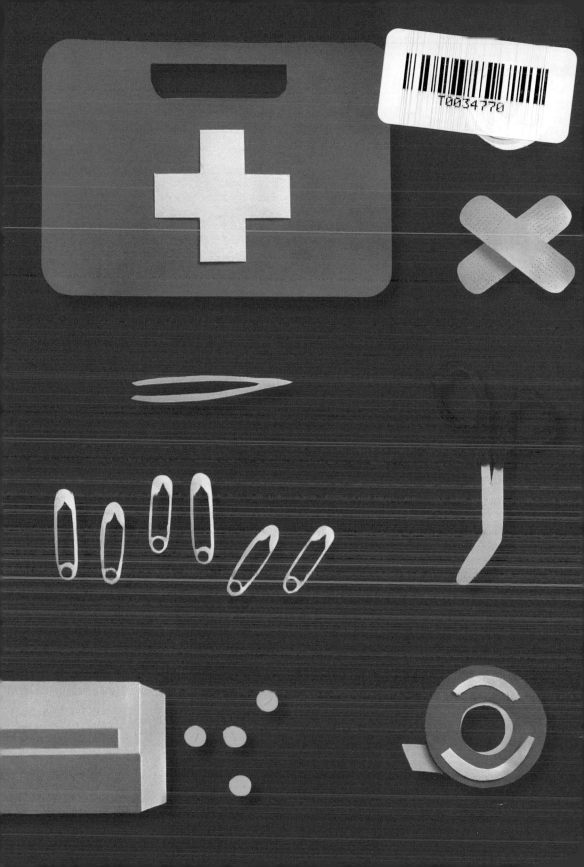

T0034770

Creative Flow

Roberta Bergmann

Creative Flow

40 Prescriptions for Tapping
Your Creative Impulses

SCHIFFER
PUBLISHING

4880 Lower Valley Road • Atglen, PA 19310

Other Schiffer Books on Related Subjects:
Artists Write to Work, Kate Kramer, ISBN
978-0-7643-5649-0
Floral Doodling Handbook, Julie Adore, ISBN
978-0-7643-6183-8
The Little Drawing Workshop, Magali Cazo &
Michel Lauricella, ISBN 978-0-7643-6185-2

Originally published as *Kopf Frei für den kreativen
Flow* by Haupt Verlag, Bern, Switzerland © 2018
by Haupt Bern
Translated from the German by Simulingua, Inc.

Library of Congress Control Number: 2021948083

Cover design by Ashley Millhouse
Back cover photos by Nina Sieverding, Roberta
Bergmann, Fabian Nilius, and Ulrike Möltgen.
Type set in PT Sans

ISBN: 978-0-7643-6308-5
Printed in India

Published by Schiffer Publishing, Ltd.
4880 Lower Valley Road
Atglen, PA 19310
Phone: (610) 593-1777; Fax: (610) 593-2002
Email: Info@schifferbooks.com
Web: www.schifferbooks.com

For our complete selection of fine books on this
and related subjects, please visit our website at
www.schifferbooks.com. You may also write for a
free catalog.

Schiffer Publishing's titles are available at special
discounts for bulk purchases for sales promotions
or premiums. Special editions, including
personalized covers, corporate imprints, and
excerpts, can be created in large quantities for
special needs. For more information, contact the
publisher.

We are always looking for people to write books
on new and related subjects. If you have an idea
for a book, please contact us at proposals@
schifferbooks.com.

Author's Note:
Together with the publisher's editing department,
I have decided to simplify the salutations and
declined gender-specific terms. Furthermore,
when I write about "creative people,"
"participants," and so on, I am always referring to
their function and not their gender.

Foreword *Who Is This Book For?* ---------------------------- 8

What Is Creativity? *A Brief Introduction* ---------------- 10

Questionnaire about Creative Types --------------- 14

       16

Which Creative and Working Type Are You? ------- 22

How to Start ---------- 24

1. Status Quo ------------------------------ 25
2. The Place ------------------------------ 26
3. Workplace -------------------- 26
4. The Battle Plan --------------------------- 27
5. Distractions
6. Get Started -------------------------------- 27

40 Prescriptions -------- 28 --------- 30

       32

№1   Just Get Started
№2   Or Do You Prefer to Plan? ----------------- 34
№3   Finding the Right Theme ----------------- 38
№4   Stash of Materials: Treasure Hoards ------------- 40
№5   Ask Your Way through Your Future Project
№6   Act Like a Child --------------------- 42
№7   Think in the Opposite Way ---------- 44
№8   Sources of Inspiration ---------- 46
№9   Rendezvous with Yourself ---------- 48
№10 Chaos! ---------- 50 -------- 54
№11 Recombine Things ------ 52
№12 Riches of Variation ----------- 56
№13 Use Your Subconscious --------- 58 ---- 60
№14 Try It Out Mathematically
№15 Provoke, Rebel: Time for Wild Ideas! ------------ 62
№16 Change Your Perspective ---------------- 64
№17 Hermit or Team Player? ---------- 68
№18 Things Do Happen by Chance --- 66
№19 Hang in There; Keep Going! ------------ 70
№20 And Now: Take a Break! ------------------ 72
№21 Sparring Partner
№22 Be Interdisciplinary ---------------- 74

№23   Take the Elevator   80

76

78

№24   Practice, Practice, Practice
№25   Tell Stories   82
№26   No Dogmatism, Please!   84   86
№27   Experiment
№28   Broadening Your Horizons   88
№29   Improvise   90   92
№30   Keep It Simple
№31   Intuition or: the First Idea   94
№32   Selective Perception   96
№33   Visualize Ideas   98
№34   Role Models & Guiding Figures
№35   Research Spirit & Inventive Spirit   100
№36   Humor   102
№37   Get Yourself Moving   104
№38   Surrealism   106
№39   Find Analogies
№40   Thinking Outside the Box   110   108

First Aid for Blocking   112

Recognizing & Analyzing Blocks   114
№1   Be Brave, Jump In   116
№2   Get Out of Your Comfort Zone   120   118
№3   The Right Timing   122
№4   There's No Such Thing as Perfection!   124
№5   Find Rituals   126
№6   Turn Negative into Positive   128
№7   Willpower, Perseverance & Continuity
                                130   132
№8   Support   134
№9   Set Boundaries
№10   Time Out for Body and Spirit
№11   Overcome Obstacles   140   138
№12   A Restart
№13   Appreciate Your Worth
№14   Classify Criticism Objectively   142
№15   Stop! Pull the Emergency Brake   144

Appendix   148

150   146

Thanks!   151
Recommended Reading   152
Sources
Photos and Illustrations   153
Index   157

Foreword

This book is for all creative people who want to enhance their creativity even more! It's a book to let you "be inspired." It's intended to motivate, activate and inspire new ideas and approaches in creative work.

So, let's get going. Take this book, sit down so that you are relaxed, and immerse yourself in my forty practice exercises and methods which I present to you in the first part of the book. Let yourself be inspired by it and be brave and simply try out the tasks without any preconceptions! You will learn a lot about yourself and especially about your way of working, and in the end, you'll be richer in experience.

> "Creativity requires something like courage."
>
> Henri Matisse, painter

This book is for those who want to use their creativity in a focused manner and who suspect that "This in-volves something more!" I want to give you new input so that you can get out of your usual comfort zone. Venture into uncharted territory with the help of the book, because it will produce more innovative and more individual results than before.

And should you ever go astray, in the second part of the book, I have put together fifteen first aid tips to get out of your creative lull and get rid of those doubts, killer phrases, and mental blocks. I will explain how you can get yourself out of such dead-end situations, get the better of your "inner Schweinehund"—your baser instincts—and how you can manage to become more effective, be able to set your priorities, to be more attentive in the creative process, and thus to be more attentive to yourself.

But what kind of creativity is this book really about? For me, creativity is every form of new creative thinking and acting in the classic creative fields, such as the liberal arts, design (including photography, drawing, illustration, layout, drafting, creative and creative/design thinking), creative writing, dance and acting, making music, cooking and baking, handicrafts, goldsmithing, carpentry, and arts and crafts.

With this book, I'm addressing the greater "DIY community," all those who see themselves as do-it-yourselfers. My practice exercises can help you do things like come up with a business idea, write a blog, make a small film, take a series of photos, or draw illustrations for a story.

But it doesn't have to involve such complex projects! You are being just as creative when you come up with a recipe for homemade cake, cook without a recipe, sew a new piece of clothing, crochet a throw with unusual patterns, or redecorate your own

---

Do it yourself. (DIY for short):

This describes activities that amateurs can do without professional help, such as those associated with do-it-yourself handicrafts like making repairs or improvements, recycling or upcycling, or creating and inventing.

apartment. No matter what your creative intentions, this book can help you to explore your limits, to push your creativity and to persevere—an important requirement!

Just like my previous publication (*The Basics of Design*, Haupt Verlag, Bern 2016), this book does not provide any results that you can work towards with the help of instructions. Rather, I would like to motivate you (and all other readers) to creatively draw upon yourself, to trust yourself to be more creative without looking left and right and wondering, "how others do it" or "how to do it right." The practice exercises in the book are described in very broad terms, so that you will be able to apply them to as many general themes as possible and to give you a lot of freedom in performing them.

With all the immediacy of information today, you will be overwhelmed with creative ideas when engaging in DIY work and creativity. This can be very intimidating and can sometimes have a blocking effect on your own brainstorming.

What is important is to detach yourself from all these (preconceived) images so that you are able to be freely creative again yourself. This way, it's possible in the future to actually generate innovative, new ideas.

It's often assumed that everything has already been thought of, written about, and invented before; that there are no more new ideas, only combinations of the existing ones. I don't really want to believe

> "Ideas are like rabbits. You get a couple and learn how to handle them, and pretty soon you have a dozen."
>
> John Steinbeck, author

that. I think it has simply become a lot harder to come up with something new *because* so much has already been thought of, written about, and invented. But in my opinion, this is not to be excluded.

Finally, one more important note: being creative is work and by no means always easy. And it takes time. Creativity takes practice. It's from this that experience grows, and with it, you become faster and better, and the ideas intensify. Soon you will have more ideas than time to put them into effect—something that I experience all the time. So far, I have never had to fear that I wouldn't be able to think of anything more (something many believe). Rather, I am sad that I don't have the time to pursue all of my ideas and carry out each one!

With this in mind, I wish you as many new ideas as possible during and after reading this book; a boost to your creativity and, above all, fun—perhaps the most important prerequisite of all!

P.S. If you want to, you can ask questions on this subject in my Facebook group "KreativPERSCRIPTIONe" ("Creative Prescriptions") or share your creative results with like-minded people and the DIY community there, at; https://www.facebook.com/groups/KreativPERSCRIPTIONe.

What Is Creativity?

The word "creativity" *(Latin creare = to create anew, to invent something, to create/ generate)* has been somewhat overused in recent years. It has been used in some more or less appropriate contexts, and there is a range of definitions. There are also innumerable publications on techniques for creativity and the theme of "generating ideas."

In general, the word is used when it involves the emergence of new ideas, in the sense of innovation and new creation. You can find it wherever a person is creatively engaged. This can be in everyday situations (such as raising children, work, interaction with others), in technological and economic contexts (such as investments, entrepreneurship, inventions), in scientific professional fields (such as discoveries that change society positively or negatively, like a cure for cancer or the atomic bomb), or in handicraft and artistic contexts (such as carpentry, design, cooking and baking, crea-tive writing, handwork, interior design, music, and the performing and liberal arts).

People are said to be "creative" when they are able to think unconventionally (i.e., freely), to break out of predefined and solidified structures, to tread new and unknown paths, to creatively draw from within themselves, and to experiment in order to come up with new ideas, associations, and solutions. In this way, they are able to question what already exists and then to change it, to design something in the broadest sense according to their

> "You can't produce anything interesting if you're not interested in anything."
>
> Will Gompertz, author

ideas, and thus to solve any potential prblem (such as for people in general). This creative behavior is mostly linked to a natural and passionate curiosity about a theme and to an urge to research that the creative person *must* pursue. And that means that every person who wants to be creative will also become so, because they are seriously, passionately, and persistently pursuing a specific goal of their own free will. This is what we call intrinsic motivation. And people who don't want to be creative, also won't become successfully creative either.

The idea that there is such a thing as innate creativity, the concept of an idea of genius, has been strongly questioned by the research on creativity done by **Robert W. Weisberg**, for example. According to his thesis, there is no such thing as divine inspiration, nothing magical or any inherited genius. Rather, he speaks much more of intelligent people who use their intelligence to roll knowledge over and over again in their heads; who combine it anew; who adopt different perspectives; who stick to the problem/ theme more persistently than others do, in order to, consciously or subconsciously, ultimately come up with the creative idea or the solution to the problem. The thought process carried out this way is free, associative, and logical, and so there is nothing "extraordinary" or magical about it.

As detailed in the research results of psychology professor **Michael A. West,** a person who is capable of creative and innovative behavior, more or less compri-

Personality:	Cognitive Prerequisites:	Working Style:
- appreciates cultural values; - has motivation, commitment, authenticity; - has a certain (technical) knowledge and broad education; - is non-conformist; - is open, has its own spirit, is spontaneous, flexible, self-confident, willing to take risks, curious, resilient, ambitious and has perseverance.	- understands complex issues; - does not make immediate judgments; - good memory; - can break out of thought patterns; - is able to use brain areas correctly and comprehensively (left as well as right hemisphere and different brain regions simultaneously).	- friendly, encouraging, outstanding, supportive, motivating, empathetic; - making space and time for creativity; - independent action; - supporting new ideas; - active listening; very good communication; - high tolerance for frustration; - sure judgment.

ses the qualities listed in this box in his or her personality, his or her thinking, and his or her work style, and thereby stands out from other, non-creative people.

One key concept in creativity research is lateral thinking (Latin latus = side), established by the cognitive scientist **Edward de Bono**, among others. Colloquially also called "Querdenken" in German, lateral thinking is a creative problem-solving method that ignores traditional, rational logic (here: vertical thinking) and approaches problems from an unorthodox direction. In this process, the person makes so-called creative leaps of thought, leaving behind the usual thought patterns and branching off in new (illogical, slightly crazy, etc.) directions and into the unknown. Seen from these new perspectives, it's often possible to solve seemingly unmanageable problems. De Bono describes it like this: "Instead of digging deeper, you are digging a new hole." This principle is the basis of many techniques for creativity.

Another key term, which differs from lateral thinking only in terms of content by a matter of nuances, was coined by the psychologist **Joy Paul Guilford**: divergent thinking (Latin: *divergere* = to strive to be apart). It stands for an open, unsystematic and playful approach to problems and projects. J.P. Guilford called this conventional way of thinking "convergent" (Latin *convergere* = inclining towards one another).

It's astonishing that creative people are not naturally omni-creative, but rather they can very rarely or never be creative in more than one area at the same time. The psychologist Howard Gardner describes this as "being creative in X," thus not "being creative in general." On the one hand, this is surely due on the one hand to preparatory training or education, and on the other hand to personal interests. Besides this, setting priorities can help a person be really good in an area.

Creativity is not measurable, precisely because it's so complex and can be defined in so many different ways. Every person is unique. A person's creativity can only be measured by their creative ideas and results. At the same time, creativity cannot be planned and very rarely occurs consciously. I don't sit down at my desk and say to myself: "Okay, now I am being creative!" Nevertheless, you can always distinguish among the same five phases of the creative process (even if only in retrospect). This classification was defined by psychologist and happiness researcher **Mihály Csíkszentmihályi**, who coined the term "flow", like this: initially, you are in the preparation phase. During this phase, you are approaching the problem, the task, the project.

You actively adopt your own stance, define the situation (for yourself), and have an approxi- mate idea of what you

> "All the good ideas I ever had came to me while I was milking a cow."
>
> Grant Wood, painter

on it overnight" before arriving at an important solution/decision. The incubation phase is replaced by the phase of insight. If the subconscious has done enough work, we usually surprise ourselves, even in relaxed situations between subconscious and conscious, with an "aha! moment" that seems to come out of nowhere. Whether when you are taking a shower or brushing your teeth, just before going to sleep or just after waking up, daydreaming during a break, suddenly there is a solution, a new path, an insight. In Phase 4, the evaluation, you can now review your inspiration for its feasibility. Attention: this is where your mindset needs to be changed! An evaluation is not an inventive-creative action, but a purely critical-rational action, and a convergent mind is required. If you

Flow:
describes a mental state of complete immersion and concentration, which is sometimes even described as hypnotic and trance-like. You become completely absorbed in an activity that seems to go off by itself, which seems very exhilarating to you, regardless of which action is being performed and which professional field is involved.

want to do or what the individual goal (= optimum) should be. As soon as the preparation has been completed, Phase 2 follows, the incubation. This task can be done in the back of your head and more passively; this means that you work on it and "digest" it in your own subconscious. In the vernacular, we speak of "sleeping

think the approach you have found is feasible, the last phase, Phase 5, takes effect: working it out. From the originally fixed idea and the following reality check, you develop a solid solution that withstands all doubts and attempt to get sOmething optimum. The result has to be defended, because new ideas and innovations often have a difficult time in the beginning. They have yet to assert and prove themselves.

Sometimes the creative process takes a course that is entirely its own. In these moments, results emerge that you would not have expected. Many independent artists openly admit that, at the beginning of their creative process, they do not yet know where the journey is taking them and that they do not yet have a specific piece of work/goal in mind. Or they experiment and the result is an absolute failure. But mistakes can also be useful *(see pages 122-123)*: they either lead to new insights ("That wasn't the right way. I'll try another.") or to completely new goals ("I hadn't thought of this result! But it's interesting: I'm now concentrating on this new aspect and completely forgetting about my first approach! This is much more exciting.").

Creativity is not tied to any age. One can be actively creative in every phase of life. I'm fascinated by the German writer Ingrid Noll, for example, who published her first novel at the age of 56 (*Der Hahn ist tot* [*The Rooster Is Dead*], Diogenes, 1991). A new phase of life had begun for her at

> ## "I start with a specific intention, and then it becomes something completely different."
>
> Pablo Picasso, artist

that time; her children were out of the house, and she finally found enough time to write.

Can everyone discover their own creativity, continue to train it further, and thus improve it? I maintain that yes, anyone can do that. The prerequisites are, on the one hand, your own will and diligence, and on the other hand, an openness to go down unknown paths and try new things. Creativity techniques can help at this point. Many of these have been developed in the last few decades and some of them have been heavily hyped. Many creative people say of themselves that they don't need techniques; they draw upon themselves and are always ready. In most cases, I would also say that of myself! However, there are situations where you either get stuck due to a block or only produce conventional, similar solutions and results, but you aren't really working innovatively. Here some creativity techniques can be used to intervene very effectively, give your own creativity a leg up, and qualitatively enhance your capabilities. However, you have to bring the basis along with you; with only a technique and without intrinsic motivation you will in fact generate results, but not creative, innovative ideas.

In the following pages I will describe forty prescriptions that are based on well-known creativity techniques, or ones that I have picked out from my own work practice, to the best of my knowledge and belief, because they have proven to be useful and helpful for me.

$\longrightarrow$ 3. Insight $\longrightarrow$ 4. Appraisal $\longrightarrow$ 5. Working It Out

Questionnaire

Creative Types

WHICH CREATIVE AND WORKING TYPE ARE YOU?

The following test can help you find out who you are when you are working creatively.

Read through the following statements and the associated four possible answers. Then rate the answers by giving them from 0 to a maximum of 4 points (0 = does not apply at all, 4 = applies totally). At the same time, it doesn't matter whether you give all the answers the same number of points, whether you rank them (1 to 4 points) or whether you mix them up wildly (such as 2 points one time, 4 points two times, and 0 points one time).

Important: answer spontaneously and don't think too long about the answers.

TEST

Statements and Their Possible Answers	0–4 P.	Sym.
1. When I start a new project,		
… I think it over thoroughly and for a long time, then I decide on a topic based on my gut feeling.		Δ
… I consider the costs and benefits in advance, what goal it's pursuing, and whether it has any chance of success. I also google it to see whether it already exists.		∫
… A thousand things come to mind, so I get started right away		¤
… I create a written concept including a project description, a schedule and a list of materials. Besides this, I ask myself if I can manage it alone or if I should seek qualified help.		•
2. If I am working creatively/am being creative, I would describe myself as:		
…Controlled, systematic, fully involved, in between self-doubting;		•
… Forgetting about myself and zealous, free, impulsive, chaotic, happy;		¤
… Very enthusiastic and convinced, unstructured, erratic, excited;		Δ
… Thoughtful, somewhat doubtful, deliberative, fact-oriented, goal-oriented.		∫
3. If I create something new through creativity		
… I think only about my own reaction. First and foremost, I must like it!		¤
… I would like to be appreciated for it. I achieve this by doing my best, paying attention to quality, and appreciating it myself.		•
… I know that there is a market for it, and I have a strategy for how to make it known.		∫
… I firmly believe that it will change something, and I already have a lot of ideas as to how I will introduce it to the world.		Δ

4. If someone asks me if we want to set up something creative together

... I consider whether the person will be able to advance and complement me with her or his capabilities. I make sure that he or she meets my requirements.	●
... I am happy that I have company and that we can work creatively together! In any case, it will be better than working alone!	Δ
... I think that I would still prefer to do it alone.	¤
... I will do that when it helps the work.	∫

5. If something unexpected (such as disruption, change, surprise, correction of the task/briefing) happens in the creative process

... it doesn't bother me; rather, I use it and play with it.	¤
... I become totally out of sorts and I wonder what I did wrong. After the first shock, I reposition and re-focus and try to move on.	●
... I become surprised, because I didn't expect this. I continue working, without letting myself get any more annoyed.	∫
... I think about pursuing the new impulse, and ultimately, I take several pathways. That certainly can't hurt.	Δ

6. When I'm pressed for time

... I think about how I can save time so that I can finish on time.	∫
...I just keep going. There are more important things than deadlines!	¤
... I encourage myself and assure myself that I will still make it.	Δ
... I easily become panicked. I'm not good at dealing with time pressure.	●

7. When I'm blocked and can't be creative

... I keep working anyway; it will just turn out mediocre or, in the worst case, nothing will come of it. In any case, I won't let that stop me from continuing.	¤
... I analyze what could be the cause and work on it.	●
... I consider stopping the work completely.	Δ
... I know that it won't last forever. I'll use the time until then for other things.	∫

8. Which word best describes you as a spontaneously creative person?

Enthusiastic	Δ
Persistent	●
Creative	¤
Conceptual	∫

9. I deal with fiascoes as follows:

I am hard on myself and wonder at which point I should have acted differently so that the work would have been a success. As appropriate, I'll do better next time and learn from the mistakes.	•
I had already suspected that this might happen. I take note of it calmly and do not allow myself to be further distracted by it. It even motivates me for the next time!	∫
I get pretty down and it will to take a while before I can get active again.	¤
Maybe it would be better if I should stop.	Δ

10. I react to project or job inquiries as follows:

If necessary, I will have the request sent to me in writing and ask questions to make sure that I have understood everything correctly. I try to put myself in my counterpart's shoes.	•
If I find the request good, I analyze it carefully and try to develop a professional business idea from it. If I can't identify with it, I quickly say no.	∫
I do my best and hope that the interested person will appreciate my creativity. I orient myself to his or her wishes.	Δ
I'm not interested in inquiries. I work first and foremost for myself. If a buyer can ultimately be found, okay, but I don't have to rely on that.	¤

Please count up your points now, sorted according to the symbols, and enter them in the evaluation box.

The creative type for which you have the most points is that one that most likely applies to you (including behavior patterns, values and principles, skills and limits). Using the Creative Type coordinate system (*see page 21*), you can then visually locate yourself among the different character positions: Using the two-dimensional representation that results when you connect all four point results with a line so as to form a square, you can see where there most likely will be intersections among the creative types, and where there may be a focal point.

¤ = TYPE 1	• = TYPE 2	Δ = TYPE 3	∫ = TYPE 4
.... Points	.... Points	.... Points	.... Points

THE CREATIVE TYPES

¤ —TYPE 1: ARTISTIC & REBELLIOUS

You live out your creativity in an inventive way and prefer to remain alone when It comes to doing the work. You want to express yourself personally by what you do.

Your qualities are: rather extroverted, self-confident, open-minded, spontaneous, impulsive, autonomous/independent, non-conformist, freedom-loving, passionate, chaotic, intuitive, self-doubting, bursting with ideas, often self-taught, willing to take risks, experimental.

This Is how you might appear to the outside world (positive +, neutral °, negative -):

+ Creative, crazy and Individualistic (not conforming to the norm), decisive, seeking discourse;
° Provocative, radical, improvising;
− Self-contained, egoistic, ego-centric, lonely, shy of contact, aloof.

• -TYPE 2: VIRTUOUS & PERFECTIONIST

You passionately build your creativity upon self-acquired knowledge and your experience. You want to be the best at what you do.

Your qualities are: objective, rather introverted, reliable, loyal, punctual, determined, questioning, passionate, rule-following, responsible, law-abiding, safety-loving, planning, thoughtful, a team player (but makes high demands on the team), disciplined.

This is how you might appear to the outside world (positive +, neutral °, negative -):

+ Resilient, orderly, self-confident, takes an overview, respectful, leader, organizer;
° Rational, systematic, controlling;
− Pedantic, dogmatic, inflexible, instructive.

You let yourself be guided by your heart's desires and your feelings in your creative work. You want to change the world a bit with the work that you do.

Your qualities are: people-oriented, sensitive, rather introverted, compassionate, utopian thinking, spontaneous, crazy, open and a team player, flexible, considerate, in need of harmony, avoids conflict, optimistic, sociable, affectionate, high-level giving quality, emotive, fair, willing to compromise, stirring, unrealistic, chaotic.

This is how you might appear to the outside world (positive +, neutral °, negative -):

+   Lively, enthusiastic, passionate, sociable, warm-hearted;
°   Quickly inspired, emotional;
–   Dreamy, irrational, unstructured, naive, not acting purposefully, excessive, gullible.

∫-TYPE 4: PRAGMATIC & RATIONAL

Your creativity is based on factual considerations and decisions. Along the lines of: what makes sense and what does the world need? You take it on!

Your qualities are: objective, planning, down-to-earth, safety-loving, thoughtful, questioning, interpretive, rationally decisive, subordinate, decisive, able to give/take criticism, reflective, judgmental, intellectual, minimalistic, environmentally conscious, a team player, orderly.

This is how you might appear to the outside world (positive +, neutral °, negative -):

+ Educated and knowledgeable, disciplined, rational, reasonable, factual, informed and well prepared;
° Knowing, controlled, sober, realistic;
– Less willing to compromise, skeptical, brusque, pessimistic, strict.

Note: Your creative type results are, of course, more of an ideal image. The typology is somewhat exaggerated, and it's not a blueprint of who you are. It's more likely that you are a good mixture of various creative types.

The test is primarily intended to sharpen your view of yourself, make you think about the statements, to motivate you and sensitize you.

The sensitization relates, on the one hand, to yourself and your actions and on the other hand, to your behavior towards others. This test may perhaps arouse your understanding of other personality types that you find around you and it may offer you an explanation of why your fellow human beings behave and work "differently" than you do.

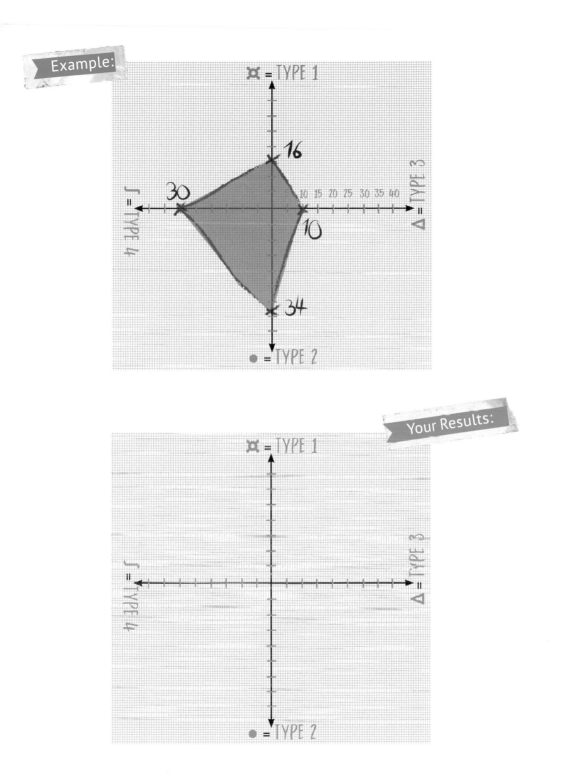

Example:

Your Results:

HOW TO START

✕✕✕✕✕✕✕✕✕✕✕✕✕✕✕✕✕✕✕✕✕✕✕

To be able to develop your creativity fully, you have to recognize what individual requirements you have and what you need so that you can be optimally creative! Based on evaluation from the questionnaire, you now know which creative type you are. That will help you in the next step to understand why it's necessary to meet certain individual prerequisites for yourself, so that you can get into a creative flow.

Yet, before you are ready to forget eveything around you and get started, here are a few points that you should take note of and define for yourself, in order to create an optimal and effective starting situation for your creativity.

1. STATUS QUO

First of all, make yourself aware of what starting situation you are in right now. This is your status quo! What do you want to set about doing creatively and what do you require to be successful with it?

1) Formulate a goal! *A clear (written) formulation helps you to visualize what it is that you really want.*

2) Describe your future, ideal work or project situation to reach your goal, such as how much time you need, whether there are other people involved, *whether the goal needs a specific place, what kind of budget you have, what materials you will need.*

Tip: If you don't like to write out a text, draw your answers as a mind map or make yourself a vision board *(see page 32.).*

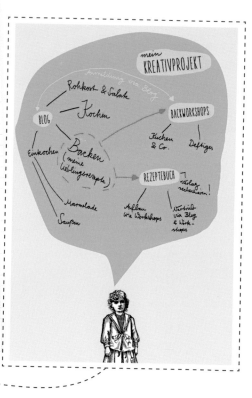

2. THE PLACE

The place where you are creative has a great influence on yourself and your actions. You should therefore make a conscious decision about a location. It should be a place where you can be optimally creative and do it without distractions.

The following options are available, depending on your activity and space requirements: *an office, studio, workshop, public space (such as a library, cafe), co-working space, workroom, apartment, on the train & bus (such as for commuters), a rehearsal room, rehearsal stage, studio, the outdoors, and so on.* Another decisive factor when choosing a location is whether you like to work alone or in a team or with other people.

The acoustics of the place also play a role: if you are sensitive to noise, you will not be able to be creative in an open-plan office! In a small communal office, you may be annoyed when other people are on the phone or listening to music (or it's annoying to others when you are on the phone or listening to music). How do you deal with noise from outside (such as from construction sites, background noises such as humming devices, air conditioning, etc.)? Visuals

also play an important role in the choice of location: Do you need a lot of light for your work? If so, is artificial light the right thing for you or does it have to be daylight? Do too many windows distract you because you often look outside and let yourself get distracted this way? Or do you need this "broad vision"? What furnishings do you need? Do you prefer to work in well-lighted, tidy, and spartanly furnished places, or do you like it chaotically creative with lots of working materials, shelves, and equipment all around your workplace? At what ambient temperature do you feel comfortable? Do you get too cold or too hot quickly? And one final, but not insignificant question: Are you ready to pay something for a place of work, and if so, what budget do you have available?

3. WORKPLACE

When you've found a place to be creative, take the next step and set up an optimal workplace for yourself and your project. Think it all over and decide:

1) How do you want to work? *For example, standing up, sitting, moving freely (such as at a desk, on a swivel chair, on a sitting ball chair, at a workbench, at a standing desk, on a sofa).*

2) What do you need around you or what disturbs and interrupts your creative process and should be banned? *For example, collection of materials (your stash of treasured materials), books, bookshelves, tools (such as brushes, pliers, wooden spoon, saw, glue), devices (such as a printer, scanner, cordless screwdriver, oven), radio/music, tea/coffee, telephone, computer, internet, other furniture.*

Tip: If you intend to use certain materials, think about having enough of everything available in your workplace. Nothing is more annoying than when you are in the middle of your work process and suddenly you don't have the things that you need to continue. The same applies for maintaining your devices: always keep a reserve of spare parts and refill materials (such as batteries, ink cartridges).

4. THE BATTLE PLAN

Your workplace is set up and there is nothing more you need. You can get started! You can use the following methods to avoid starting out like a chicken without its head. Perhaps they will help you to be more structured and thus more efficient in the creative process.

Write yourself a to-do list for today! *Be realistic and think about what you want to achieve as your goal(s) for today. At the same time, calmly plan for everything, including the non-creative tasks that have a high priority. But don't forget your creative goals, and plan in enough time!*

Enter all activities into a timetable for this day! *This helps you get things done, because this way you are now committed to doing them. Things don't have to be detailed; it may be enough to plan for time periods of several hours or to divide the day into mornings and afternoons (see the subject of "Time Planning," page 120).*

5. DISTRACTIONS

You're in the middle of the process and it's going really well; you have a flow! Unfortunately, you are being disturbed for the third time in an hour and every time it tears your thought process to shreds. Therefore, pay attention to the sources of interference and distracting traps and keep on switching them off, if necessary.

Sources of disturbance include such things as telephone calls, incoming messages and the noises they make (computer, telephone, tablet), colleagues/employees (ask them to please be considerate), or a ringing doorbell (the postal service, couriers).

Distraction traps include such things as emails, social networks, less important tasks (neither urgent nor important—review your priorities), conversations (which are not part of the process), and "displacement" activity (such as tidying up, sorting things out).

However, certain distractions are okay, such as a glance out the window, stretching exercises (actually important for in between during sedentary activities!), eating, drinking, and toilet breaks (many forget about that when they are in the midst of a flow or under stress).

6. GET STARTED

Brooding about the "How to start" is all well and good (and important). Nevertheless, you shouldn't forget about actually starting! Otherwise there is a risk that the whole preparatory process will degenerate into pure distraction. So first, just get started (see Prescription № 1 on page 30).

40 Prescriptions

JUST GET STARTED

As already stated in the "How to Start" chapter, one way of starting a creative project is to simply start in without thinking about it a whole lot beforehand. There is the saying, "The best way to get something done is to start it." But this beginning can be difficult, and this can be true for both the rational and the perfectionist creative types. They are afraid of doing something wrong already when they are taking the first step. To calm yourself down and take the wind out of the sails of any such assumption—which comes from having too-high expectations for yourself—think this: Who is so ingenious that they produce ideas that are "ready for printing" with the first line, the first thought? Hardly anyone!

An English proverb says, "How do you eat an elephant? One bite at a time." That means nothing more than "Don't be afraid of tasks that seems to be over-dimensional! Try to solve them step by step. Start with step 1, then step 2, etc."

What could the beginning actually look like? That depends entirely on your creative project! You can start with a brainwriting—write yourself a list. You can record your ideas, or you can start directly with the task without sketching anything out beforehand and start working it out. This creates a first draft that you can analyze and then improve on. Another small tip: quietly leave what you've done alone at first, for a few hours or a day, before you look at it once again with a bit of time perspective.

#

#Brainwriting
#ToDoList
#IdeaSketch
#JustStart
#EatAnElephant
#NoFear
#Collage
#Spontaneous
#TrialAndError
#MichelGondry
#CentrePompidou
#UsineDeFilmsAmateurs

Photo from a collage workshop where the participants were given the task of spontaneously gluing on new pictures from old magazines.

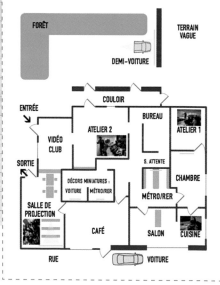

LE PLAN DE L'USINE DE FILMS AMATEURS

FORÊT

TERRAIN VAGUE

DEMI-VOITURE

ENTRÉE

COULOIR

BUREAU

ATELIER 2

ATELIER 1

VIDÉO CLUB

SORTIE

S. ATTENTE

CHAMBRE

DÉCORS MINIATURES : VOITURE MÉTRO/RER

MÉTRO/RER

SALLE DE PROJECTION

CAFÉ

SALON

CUISINE

RUE

VOITURE

Filmmaker **Michel Gondry** gives every museum visitor to the **Centre Pompidou** in Paris the opportunity to spend three hours making their own short film, without any previous expertise. In his exhibition/installation *The Home Movie Factory* (*L'Usine de Films Amateurs*), eight to twenty visitors get together as a film group who will make a short film in the space of three hours, following a set of guidelines specified by Gondry. Ten film sets and all kinds of film equipment are set up on site for them to do this. At the end, the movie will be shown in the exhibit, and each participant will receive a personal copy to take home with them.

PRACTICE: *Just get started with:*

_____

(enter your project title here).

The title of a creative project, as the heading for your future work, can already provide you with a lot of content. It can inspire you, give you a feeling for the subject matter, and stimulate your creativity. And by putting the title in writing and pronouncing it aloud (that sounds banal, but shouldn't be underestimated), it has already become a bit of reality. The first step has been taken and the first decision made.

OR DO YOU PREFER TO PLAN?

If you are the virtuoso, perfectionist creative type or the rational, pragmatic creative type, you will rather tend to make a plan before starting the practical creative work, instead of immediately plunging into the work. It's important to you to think about what your new project might look like in advance. You define a goal that makes sense to you and is also worth your time and work. You then work towards this project, using a specific plan.

There are a lot of tools available for planning a project. You can use assorted methods to structure a large project more clearly and div-ide it into milestones (small intermediate goals) *(see page 120)*.

Written or pictorial representations are more ways of organizing your time and planning your projects—and thus making the big picture apparent. Depending on what suits you better, you note down all stages of your project in a matrix, such as in a project flow chart, a written mind map, a to-do list or a calendar-based "Bullet Journal®." If you are more of the pictorial type, you can visualize your project by using a mind map or a mood board, which consists only of pictures, or you can create a vision pin board. You can, of course, also do this online and virtually: Pinterest® is great for getting your inspirations on digital pin boards.

# #

#BulletJournal
#RyderCarroll
#Vision board
#ToDoList
#MindMap
#MoodBoard
#Pinterest
#Gimmebar

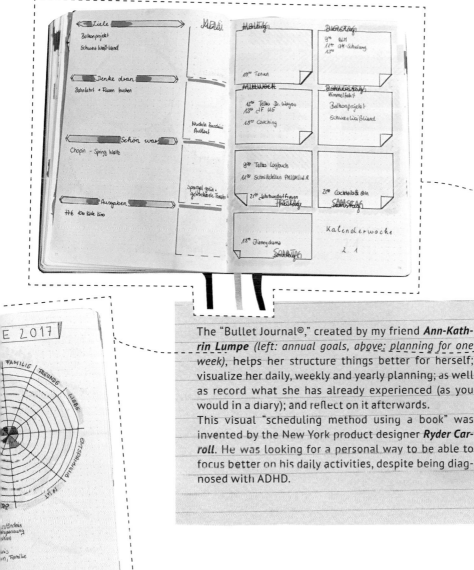

The "Bullet Journal®," created by my friend **Ann-Kathrin Lumpe** (left: annual goals, above: planning for one week), helps her structure things better for herself; visualize her daily, weekly and yearly planning; as well as record what she has already experienced (as you would in a diary); and reflect on it afterwards.

This visual "scheduling method using a book" was invented by the New York product designer **Ryder Carroll**. He was looking for a personal way to be able to focus better on his daily activities, despite being diagnosed with ADHD.

PRACTICE: *Based on the title you give your project from the practice exercise on page 31, create a vision board, a mind map, or a mood board for yourself. This should then help you get a feel for your project, give it a "face," and create an overview of the next steps for yourself.*

FINDING THE RIGHT THEME

Before you can get actively creative, you need a theme. To calm you down, remember that most of the time your theme finds you and not the other way around. You may have encountered it in a conversation the other day, or you read something interesting and then an idea came to you, along the lines of "I should definitely do something with that!" Or it has been slumbering in your mind for ages. Is there a passion that you have had since childhood? Do you have a matter close to your heart that keeps popping up in your life and wants you to take note of it? Who are your role models and why? Listen to your gut feelings and your intuition. If it interests you, grabs you, and you can convey that, it will also inspire others! Themes that get public attention and become successful are often precisely those issues that are close to your heart. Because they have an authentic impact and let you sense the author's passion.

You might want to write down the things that have made a lasting impression on you and that you would like to realize in an idea book or something similar. This can be a simple notebook that you keep, like you would a diary. Or you can make an expandable idea poster that you hang over your desk. You can also create an idea box. This can be a cigar box or an old shoebox in which you collect small things and notes that inspire you (similar to the treasure chests that some children hide under their beds).

And when it's time to find a new theme, you know where to look for inspiration.

#

#IdeaBook
#IdeaPoster
#IdeaBox
#AThemeCloseToYourHeart
#GutFeeling
#Intuition
#IdeaCollection

PRACTICE:

Take some time and create an idea collection. What are the themes that move and appeal to you? What are recurring questions and problems for which you seek answers and solutions? Write them down and do a little research about these themes. You can document all of this in an idea book, on an idea poster, on an idea wall, or in an idea box. Remember: this collection is first and foremost for you! You don't have to show it to anyone (but you can).

In my opinion, there are three ways to find an appropriate theme for a (creative) project. In addition, a mixture of the following three methods or approaches is also conceivable:

1) INTERNAL RESEARCH

A project close to your heart, intuition, gut feeling, theme from your childhood.

2) EXTERNAL RESEARCH

Your approach and interest are more the rational type; research and investigation into the theme are almost of scientific interest.

3) CATHARSIS

Spontaneous and unconscious "creation drawing from within yourself," without doing any research; bringing the subconscious to light. This method is often used in art therapy.

Once you have found a theme, it's important to bring it into being using your own resources and ideas. One way to internalize the theme is to come up with a "mission statement." This is your little manifesto, formulated as a crisp headline and instructions (just for you); you write it down on a piece of paper that you cannot easily overlook (such as stuck on the bathroom mirror, on the inside of your apartment door or hanging above your desk).

Set up my own fashion label ♡

#Research
#Catharsis
#MissionStatement
#ManifestationQuotes
#Questionnaire

PRACTICE: *Have you found a theme/project that you want to work towards? Formulate a target sentence, a so-called "mission statement," write it on 8.5x11 paper or larger (in headline size), and hang it up where you can see it every day!*

PRACTICE:

If you don't know exactly what themes are closest to your heart and what moves you, you can take your time in a quiet moment and answer the following questions. They might shed light on what is important to you and perhaps guide you towards your future project.

> *What is your favorite movie, book, series, song/music, food, activity, work of art/artist — and above all, why?*

> *What would you do if you had only one more year to live?*

> *Which thoughts and memories give you strength?*

> *What is your worst nightmare; what is your most fantastic dream?*

> *What makes you the happiest/saddest?*

> *What have been the greatest events and most wonderful encounters and friendships in your life so far; what were your successes/failures?*

> *What do you want to convey to others with your work? What do you want to pass on? What should remain behind of you when you are no longer there?*

> *Which issues (for example, social) concern you, and why?*

STASH OF MATERIALS: TREASURE HOARDS

#CollectionOfMaterials
#CreativeHamster
#CreativeStash
#Props
#JuliGudehus

Man is known to be a hunter and gatherer. In particular, the creative people among us like to collect things, regardless of whether they are thoughts and ideas for projects, or something more tangible in the form of materials—everything can be of interest for later projects. It's very helpful to build up a stock or stash of materials. You should just be careful not to let yourself get cluttered up and to clean out your hoarded stash of treasures from time to time.

A box full of found pieces, a range of beautiful papers, notebooks, brightly colored textiles and scraps of fabric, rare stamps and glossy images, antique dolls from the flea market, shadow boxes full of all kinds of stuff, books, boxes of buttons in all shapes and colors, old magazines, music, film, ribbon, picture frames, various seals, paints, and pens—anything and everything can inspire you and remind you that "Oh yes, I wanted to do something with that!" And when the day comes for a new project *(see page 36),* then you know where to look!

 What interests you in the creative sense? Do you already have a passion for collecting? If so, can you use this for your creativity? Which materials would you like to work with one day? Collect things that you like because of their haptics, aesthetics, smell, taste, appearance, idea/concept, and things that inspire you. Do something with them!

Or go to the flea market or a supplies store (such as an arts and craft supplies store, home improvement store, packaging store) and look around with your eyes open to see whether you find something that you like and that inspires you to work with it.

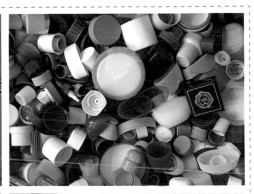

Designer **Juli Gudehus** has one of the greatest collections of materials I know. In her Berlin apartment, there are finely sorted rolls of paper and wallpaper, and a decorative stash for sticky tape enthusiasts hangs over the desk. And in the study, there is a whole shelf full of colorful boxes and binders, sorted according to theme, that have aroused the collector's interest because of their material qualities and design. One box contains several binders in which the designer has collected sheets of toilet paper motifs from all over the world. In another box there are plastic caps from cans and small bottles. And in the next box you will find all kinds of international operating instructions.

ASK YOUR WAY THROUGH YOUR FUTURE PROJECT

Once you have found a theme that you want to work with, it's important to fill in the contents. In this process, you can use the W (or H or F) questions to get to the bottom of your chosen theme. W questions are open-ended questions, which means that you cannot answer them with yes or no. These questions can be: Who? Whom? Whom? Whose? How? Where? When? Which? What? Whereby? With what? About what? Where to? For what reason? Why? How so? For what? What about? For what? In what way? From where? For what reason? What from? If necessary, you can make the questions more specific: How many? How often? How far?

For example, imagine that you're writing a story for a children's book. As a basis for the con-tents, you need: the theme (what?), characters (who?), location/setting (where?), a plot (all the W (or H or F) questions together). In order to delve further into the plot, you can make your questions more specific. What happens in the story? Who is involved and why? When did something happen? How did the events take place? Why did it happen? What are the consequences?

Concerning the above-noted project concept, you can ask yourself the following questions: What do I want to say with the story (such as the moral, goal)? Who is the target group for the book (children, gender, age range)? Which publisher would be appropriate for the story? How many pages do I need to tell the story?

#
#WQuestions
#Storytelling
#ChildrensBook
#Plot
#CreativeWriting
#LisaTegtmeier
#ChildhoodMemory

In her independent book project *Up'n Dörpe* (German dialect for *In the Village*), designer **Lisa Tegtmeier** has visualized her memories of her grandparents, who lived in the country. She asked herself such questions as: What specific moments with my grandparents can I remember? What traditions did they keep up when I was little? Which cooking and baking recipes did I learn about from my grandparents?

PRACTICE:
Imagine you meet a curious child who is pestering you with W questions about your current project. For every answer you give, the child has a new question.

Put yourself in this child's shoes. What are her or his questions, and how do you explain to her or him what it is that you are currently working on?

You can also visualize the questions and answers in a table or another schematic matrix.

ACT LIKE A CHILD

Children act according to the pleasure principle! When they play, they do it with total passion and curiosity. At the same time, they are so absorbed that they forget every-thing around them. Small children seem to dive into a parallel world. You can learn a lot from this childlike playing in the creative process! It's not just when you are working alone on a project that it's a good idea to take on a child's perspective at times. The private sector economy and many companies are now making use of this principle. *Kjeld Kirk Kristiansen*, the principal owner of *The Lego Group*, himself suggested the development of the "moderated process" Lego® Serious Play® (LSP) in 1996. In doing so, he brought together the advantages of children's play, the combination of free association and modeling with Lego bricks, and the concerns of the business world. LSP can be used in a moderated process by companies to find demonstrably faster solutions to problems. Besides this, it fosters innovation, improves company communications and team building.

In his work "White Washing Parade," artist *Jens Isensee* arranged a wide variety of toys together with one another. He thus created a variable and expansive installation, which is abstracted by the uniform white coloring. On the one hand, it directs the eye and arouses curiosity, and on the other hand, it awakens the viewer's desire to play.

#
#BeingAChildAgain
#SimplyPlaying
#Childlike
#Experiment
#Createchaos
#Toy
#Lego
#LSP
#LegoSeriousPlay
#KjeldKirkKristiansen
#JensIsensee

THINK IN THE OPPOSITE WAY

The headstand method is a popular means of literally turning everything in your own perspective around by 180° and questioning everything that you have thought about so far. This involves thinking in a way that is opposite to what seems logical and obvious. Most things always have two sides. The advantage of this approach is that you are forced to think about the second side of a matter/project, even if that seems absurd or uninteresting at first. The two opposing perspectives can yield unusual questions, such as: can music be toneless? Can you see a beautiful sky even though It's raining cats and dogs? Can you advertise your company positively using a bad slogan? The answers are: yes, it can and it has been done! A few examples: *John Cage* composed "4'33" in 1952; in this piece, he sat in front of his piano for 4 minutes and 33 seconds and did not play. The *Museum of Modern Art* in New York includes designer Tibor Kalman's "Sky" umbrella in its MoMA Collection. The surprise effect of this umbrella, which is now one of the design classics, is captivating. If you open it in the rain and look up, you can see a blue sky with fleecy white clouds. Author *Rüdiger Nehberg*, known as "Sir Vival," started his professional career as a baker and confectioner with his own business. Being a bit provocative (I would call it fun-loving), he formulated the slogan for his pastry shop: "Konditorei Nehberg ... There are worse ones." *Erwin Wurm*'s walk-through art installation "Fichte" (fir trees) displays over forty house-high Nordmann fir trees hanging from the ceiling.

#

#HeadstandMethod
#Opposite
#Satire
#Absurdity
#JohnCage
#MoMaNY
#TiborKalman
#RüdigerNehberg
#ErwinWurm

PRACTICE:

Take up a theme that you like and know and try to work on it while contradicting yourself. For example, write a disparaging review about it; paint a picture on the subject in a way that you would never paint, because you don't like the style. You can perhaps at the same time reduce the original "purpose" to an absurdity—for example, create a book without pages, a vessel with a hole in it, or music without a melody; bake a cake of concrete; or make a table with three legs. Look at the result, and think about what it says to you and what you can develop further from it.

SOURCES OF INSPIRATION

Basically, anything can serve to inspire you. As a creative person, the basic requirement is "Keep your eyes open!" You should always be ready to recognize impulses for your own creative work and to absorb them like a sponge. Tip: It's best to note down whatever it is immediately (in the old-fashioned way, using a notepad or sketchbook or digitally by phone, tablet, and the appropriate app, such as **Ever-note**®). An idea box *(see page 34)* can also serve as a mnemonic device for your inspirations.

Apart from the things that inspire us every day by chance and give us our own ideas, there is also the possibility of coming up with new ideas, using the stimulus word technique. To do this, look for any arbitrary piece of writing (a book, a grammar book, a dictionary, a magazine), open it at random in one place, and see which word catches your eye first. Compare this word with the theme that is on your mind.

This also works with stimulus images. Another variant is the snippet technique. For this, spread a lot of individual words or images out on a table and recombine them with one another and with your own theme. The goal of these techniques is to use seemingly arbitrary connections to stimulate divergent thinking and to generate unconventional ideas, and thus to steer your thinking in unusual directions. Even **David Bowie** used this technique; *see page 66.*

see page 66.

#

#StimulusWordTechnique
#StimulusImageTechnique
#Notebook
#Evernote
#IdeaBox
#UnusualPlaces
#WasteBecomesAMaterial
#Sustainability
#SnippetTechnique
#ChristineMayer
#Upcycling
#CradleToCradle

Designer *Christine Mayer* creates clothes from unusual second-hand textiles. The "Tilbert" jacket, for example, is sewn from recycled flour sacks, the "Freimut" shirt is made from hand-woven historical linen and "Rolltuch" linen tablecloths, while the "Luke" pants were once a duffel bag. All items of clothing are from the Mayer Peace Collection.

PRACTICE:
Visit or look around in an unusual, previously unknown place like a materials store, a workshop, or a production facility (such as a bookbindery, a factory). Take a close look at what materials people are working with on-site. What technical production processes are they using (such as on the machines)? Everything is interesting, including the waste produced there! (Industrial waste is increasingly experiencing a second lifetime through innovation and sustainability, such as upcycling and the cradle-to-cradle principle.)

RENDEZVOUS WITH YOURSELF

Is this something you know? For days (oh dear, it's been weeks), you have finally been wanting to get started on this one thing! You are full of anticipation and a zest for action. But something keeps coming up, and the project has to wait because it's "not urgent, not important enough" (such as because it's an independent project only for yourself, and not paid). There are two possibilities. Either you come to terms with the fact that you cannot do any such work during your everyday life, and you cannot get around to dealing with it (maybe it isn't important enough for you), or you consciously choose to take time for yourself, even though this could get you into difficulties in terms of time. I call this "arranging a rendezvous with yourself."

By setting a concrete date and time frame (at least four hours, at most one day) and a task that you want to complete within that time, this appointment takes on a certain seriousness and commitment, just like if you set up a date. You feel more obliged to keep the "appointment." It would be important that you do not allow any interference from outside during this rendezvous. This means that you should arrange in advance that no one calls or disturbs you ("I can't that day, I have an appointment.") or completely eliminate possible sources of disturbance for this time span. Attention: that may seem silly to you, but it's extremely important! If you were on a date or rendezvous, you wouldn't answer the phone, communicate with third parties and check your emails, would you?

You will be amazed at how much you can think about during this condensed time "for yourself," if nothing distracts you.

The principle can also be applied over a longer period of time, when you could be on "a vacation with yourself."

— SUPERMARKET
— DENTIST 02/02, 2 PM.
—TERTIG PHOTO JOB (DEADLINE FRIDAY 12 NOON)
— BE AT THE INSURANCE CO.
— WRITE SHORT STORY ("LEO FINDS WHAT MAKES HIM HAPPY")
— APPLY FOR THE GRANT (DEADLINE 03/31)
— VIENNA PHOTOGRAPHY COMPETITION (DEADLINE 04/15) LOOK FOR PHOTOS, CV

PRACTICE: *Check your calendar for a day when you don't have any appointments so far. Enter your "rendezvous with yourself" there. Think carefully beforehand what you want to achieve in the time span (stay realistic). Formulating a specific goal can be useful. Wait to see how your rendezvous goes and set additional dates if necessary. In addition, if routine helps you, you can specify a span of time on a certain day of the week, such as "Monday from 9 a.m. to 2 p.m. is always my project day." Take these appointments seriously and observe them!*

Illustrator *Christoph Niemann* always tries to set up "fixed dates with his independent projects" in addition to his commissioned work. It's better to regularly do at least a bit of independent work than to do none at all, he says. This way, the project can grow slowly but steadily. This is the way his *Sunday Sketching* was created.

CHAOS!

All creative people have experienced it already (even the orderly ones). Creative chaos sweeps through your workplace. It usually appears for the first time when you are in the middle of the discovery process: stacks of books, pens, materials, snippets of newspaper, sticky notes, tablets, laptop, smartphone, cookies, coffee cups, thermos flasks . . . Your desk is overflowing, and you end up using the surrounding counter surfaces and the floor. Creative chaos is nothing bad or something you should avoid. It's a phase in which order no longer comes first, because you are focusing on something else: the creative process.

Try to ignore the chaos and concentrate on your task until you have reached your goal. Cleaning up would just take you out of the process and distract you (and you'd like to distract yourself now, right?). Use your creative chaos and immerse yourself in your work, which appears wild from the outside.

A study by the **University of Minnesota Carlson School of Management** determined that working in a messy, chaotic room encouraged test subjects to try out new things and to come up with creative ideas in a way that would not occur in a tidy room.

Disorder and chaos also have something that is childlike and non-conformist about them; you leave the normal behind, and with it, the well-trodden pathways. "Order is good for an overview; chaos for surprises," says chemist and **Professor Dr. Hans-Jürgen Quadbeck-Seeger**, and he is right. Order makes sense for the beginning and for the end of a project, but in between there can be chaos, because it usually inspires the creative process.

#

#CreativeChaos
#Studio
#UniversityOfMinnesota
#CarlsonSchoolOfManagement
HansJürgenQuadbeck-Seeger
#DiscoveryProcess
#CreativeProcess
#FrancisBacon
#UlrikeMöltgen

Illustrator **Ulrike Möltgen** is best known for her colorful collages. She is happiest working on the floor. Her living room becomes occupied and quickly converted into a studio.

Things got a bit more intense in the attic apartment of English painter *Francis Bacon*, as photographed by *Perry Ogden*. Bacon's creative chaos took on messianic and manic traits. It was almost impossible to make out where the furniture was, and he converted the doors and walls into a large painting palette for himself.

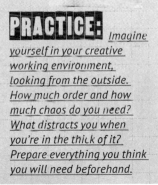

PRACTICE: *Imagine yourself in your creative working environment, looking from the outside. How much order and how much chaos do you need? What distracts you when you're in the thick of it? Prepare everything you think you will need beforehand.*

RECOMBINE THINGS

You probably know the saying "Everything has already been invented. There is nothing that doesn't exist already." Seen in this way, nobody would have to be creative anymore or take the trouble to create something that might be new. But be careful; things just aren't that simple! Of course, new things are always still being invented and created. However, this happens less frequently than before (at least it seems that way to us). This is partly due to the omnipresence of all ideas and their potential availability through the Internet. If we have an idea, we google it first. In a few seconds, we can see whether someone had the same idea (before we did). This can be paralyzing and demotivating during the discovery process.

Perhaps, in fact, you don't have to reinvent the wheel. Combining already existing ideas, systems, sectors, fields, elements, and so on can also lead to innovation. This is because to combine means to bring about the meaningful connection of at least two different things, or the spiritual linking of different ideas and thoughts.

Just take a look around: Which elements could you combine with each other in your creative playground and thus create something new? It doesn't matter at all whether this involves baking, cooking, picture making, handicrafts, design, writing, acting, or making music. This method works in all sectors! It might involve obvious combinations, but here there is a risk that you are not the first one to come up with the idea. That is why it's particularly exciting to deal with things that, at first sight, it doesn't make sense to combine!

#

#Combine
#Connection
#Link
#Interdisciplinary
#Cooking
#FoodBlog
#BerndLabetzsch
#UlrikeBrenner
#TatendrangDesign
#ToniaWiatrowski
#RobertaBergmann
#Damensalat
#RefrigeratorMagnets
#Combinatorics

 **PRACTICE:** *Take at least thirty minutes for yourself and combine two things from your everyday creative work that usually would not be combined. Experiment a bit with this until the result makes sense to you.*

The wildest combinations occur in cooking! Have you ever tried a smoked trout mousse together with beet ice cream?
Food blogger **Bernd Labetzsch** and cook **Ulrike Brenner** suggested this recipe.

Together with **Tonia Wiatrowski**, I came up with the magnetic game "Damensalat" ("Ladies' salad"), which was produced by our label **Tatendrang-Design**[®]. The aim of this game is to reassemble the four women in the pictures, each of whom has been divided into four parts. Try it out yourself; there are countless new combination options for differently dressed women. Can you discover how many variants there are?

RICHES OF VARIATION

"Variation," that is, changing an idea, a theme, or a motif in the respective creative branch (writing, music, art, sewing, cooking, performing, etc.) requires creativity, perseverance, and hard work. If you are ready to create a lot of variations, you will experience an enhancement of your creativity in the course of your creative process. And that in turn is due to your creative curve. Although, in fact, this is an individual matter for each creative type (some produce more different variations at the beginning; others become more and more productive over the duration of the creative process), nevertheless, the different process sequences have one thing in common: the longer it lasts, the more unusual variations will be born. And that is because, in part, at the beginning you are still going along your accustomed path, relying on what you can do, on techniques that you know, and combinations that you like. But once you have worked this through conceptually, you have no choice but to leave the familiar terrain (= your comfort zone) behind. And this is where things get really interesting! From the point in time when you start to experiment and try things out, completely new possibilities and results will arise that will surprise you. So I encourage you not to stop at the point when things seem to get difficult. Hold on and try to find even more variations.

# #

..MonaLisa　　　　　　#CharlotteWagner
#PetrusAkkordeon　　 #UlrikeHeidemann
#LeonardodaVinci　　 #MarieMüller
#AnitaSchwörer　　　　#Apfelhase
#JohannesEsser　　　　#SilviaKarkut
#BilleWeidenbach　　 #ChristinKloss
#RalphBergel　　　　　#DariaLitvinova
#DoroHerrmann　　　　#HannahSchrage
#GilavonMeissner　　 #TessaRath
#FelixBork　　　　　　#ArianeKrahl
#RobertaBergmann　　 #ArindaCraciun
#KathrinJebsen　　　　#ElkeErat
#KristinaBrasseler　 #Saramin
#MeikeTöpperwien　　 #EvaJaegerNilius

I had asked creative professionals via Facebook to send me their versions of the famous *Mona Lisa* by **Leonardo da Vinci**. You can find the complete list of names of these Mona Lisa interpreters on *page 154*.

USE YOUR SUBCONSCIOUS

In the creative process, your own subconscious is a factor that should not be underestimated. You shouldn't exclude it from the creative process, but instead you should become aware of your subconscious signals, interpret them, and let them flow into the creative process. This can greatly enrich yourself and your project.

For me, the best things come to mind especially during the transition between waking and sleeping. It's when I am lying in bed and it's twilight that the best titles for my books, for example, come to me. Titles that didn't want to come into my head before through brainstorming and writing. It's therefore mandatory for me to have a notepad and a pen next to my bed! Besides that, it's a good way to write down my dreams. I am a dream collector. One of my unfulfilled creative-project wishes is to write an illustrated dream book.

Daydreams—such as while you are in the shower, looking out the window, or taking a coffee break—can also be helpful to boost your creativity. Just like during the phases of falling asleep and waking up, a break from work is a time when you are relaxed and your thoughts can wander about freely. Without compulsion, you are dreaming with your eyes open, and your subconscious can take a look at and process ideas without consciously stressing yourself.

The situation is similar with selective perception: you are aware of a problem that is posed, and your brain (always looking for information) unconsciously searches for a certain pattern. At the same time, unimportant, partial aspects of your perception will fade away and your gaze will become focused.

\#
#Subconscious
#Daydream
#Dreams
#DreamDiary
#Showering
#TakingABreak
#SelectivePerception
#AnjaMillen
#LauraNagel
#Surreal

PRACTICE: *Get yourself a dream diary and put it near the place where you sleep. Write down your dreams over a longer time period after you wake up. Besides this, bring a notebook (analog or digital) along with you in your everyday life, where you can write down any flashes of inspiration, ideas, and thoughts (such as during a coffee break, at a meeting, on the train or on other public transport).*

Irish artist **Anja Millen** paints over nude photographs, and the result is that they make a dark, disturbing, and surreal impact on the viewer.

Argentine photo artist **Laura Nagel** is known for her dark, nightmarish pictures, which are created through a mixture of photography and illustration.

TRY IT OUT MATHEMATICALLY

Don't worry, I'm talking about "mathematics" in the figurative sense: adding, subtracting, multiplying and dividing are the basic types of arithmetic. You can very easily transfer them over as a method for dealing with your ideas, products, problems, tasks, projects, and so on.

Adding means combining several functions. If you were to add, for example, a clock to an illustration that you could hang in a frame on your wall, then in sum you will get a lovely wall picture and you will also know what time it is.

When you subtract, you take something away or separate out or remove partial aspects. One example is *Gestrichene Zeitung* (*Canceled Newspapers*) by artist **Timo Hoheisel**. He took one issue each of the German daily newspapers *FAZ* (*Frankfurter Allgemeine Zeitung: Frankfurt General Newspaper*), *Die Welt* (*The World*), *Die Zeit* (*The Times*), and *Süddeutsche Zeitung* (*Southern Germany Newspaper*) and subtracted their content by painting over them with white.

An example of both adding and subtracting is the German music-streaming service "Minimal." By adding or removing individual notes within a melody, its rhythmic structure will be changed. The result is a series of mathematically effective variants of one and the same theme.

When you create patterns, this involves nothing more than the multiplication of several elements within a format—by repeating the pattern, it will even go on indefinitely. This is what Swiss animation artist **Michaela Müller** does.

And if you have a longer story to tell and if you divide it by three, for example, the result is a book series in three volumes!

#Arithmetic
#Aitch
#Society6
#TimoHoheisel
#MinimalMusic
#Pattern
#RepeatedPattern
#MichaelaMüller

Illustrated clock from the *Society6* online shop by the Romanian artist *Aitch*.

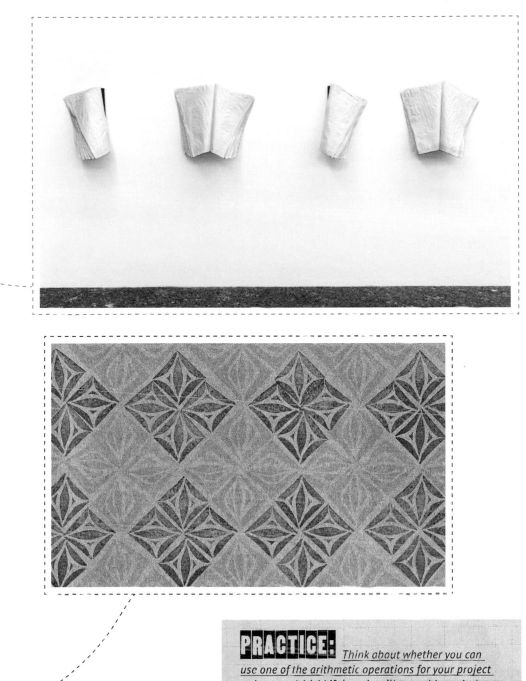

PRACTICE: *Think about whether you can use one of the arithmetic operations for your project to improve it! Add if there is still something missing; subtract if it's already too complex (and/or divide it into several projects), etc.*

PROVOKE, REBEL:
TIME FOR WILD IDEAS!

To be rebellious, to resist everyday life and the prevailing conventions, to question what exists and to be ready to make your way on a new and, above all, your own pathways—for many creative people, this is all part of their daily altercation with their own creative work. This approach requires a lot of energy and perseverance, because you will likely encounter resistance in the creative process. This can involve your own doubts or meeting "headwinds" from others. The most important thing is not to let this discourage you. A creative spirit should be allowed to be free, and innovation is often possible only under these conditions.

Provocative behavior, such as delibera-tely evoking and at the same time possibly manipulating a reaction in the viewer/consumer, is another possibility for drawing attention to yourself and your ideas. Howe-ver, you should only apply this in small doses and be careful not to harm others.

The "provocation technique" of cogni-tive scientist **Edward de Bono** also comes up in this connection. In this creativity technique, he puts existing assumptions and perspectives into question by posing "What if...?" statements. These provocative, mostly absurd assertions are intended to trigger new ways of thinking in the creative process.

Acting autonomously and, in a way, con-trary to all expectations, as well as being prepared to produce wild ideas, can be a process that will steer your creativity in new directions and thus enhance it.

#

#WildIdeas
#ProvocationTechnique
#EdwarddeBono
#LewisCarroll
#AliceinWonderland
#ElsaSchiaparelli
#Dadaism
#Surrealism
#Bowknotsweater
#SalvadorDalí

PRACTICE:

Imagine that you don't have to follow certain guidelines for one of your current projects, but would be able to approach the solution for the task freely, wildly, and autonomously. What would your path then look like, and how would it differ from the previous approach? What would you do differently? What would you leave out and what would you do instead? What would your desired result look like then? What can you derive from this for yourself?

"To begin with, I had sent my heroine straight down a rabbit-hole . . . without the least idea what was to happen afterwards . . ." This is how mathematician and author **Lewis Carroll** ex-plained the original idea for his book *Alice in Wonderland.* The rest is history. At the time of its writing, in 1865, no such "wild" children's book, which was written to be a stark contrast to the instructive Victorian children's literature of the time, had been seen before.

Fashion designer **Elsa Schiaparelli** designed sensational fashions and accessories, which were influenced by the contemporary art scene, such as the surrealists. Her talent was discovered when she was watching a fashion show in 1927, wearing her knitted bowknot sweater, which would later make her world famous.

Another wild idea arose in cooperation (*see: Creative Prescription № 17*) with world-famous artist **Salvador Dali**. This was the "shoe hat" from 1937, which was a felt hat shaped like an upside-down high-heeled shoe.

CHANGE YOUR PERSPECTIVE

##ChangeOfPerspective
#Roles
#WaltDisney
#WaltDisneyMethod
#RobertBDilts
#Misappropriate
#Herzallgaeuerliebst
#Upcycling

Changing your own perspective is another possibility for generating brand-new ideas. I'm sure you are like me. Now and then, you get stuck in your own swamp of ideas, and you don't move conceptually far enough "away from yourself" and come too quickly to what is obvious, but not to completely new ideas. But how do I change my own perspective? There are several ways. You can imagine yourself to be someone else, such as someone you admire. How would that person approach your project, and how would she or he solve the problem?

Or you take on different roles (and thus perspectives) in fictional role playing. Author **Robert B. Dilts** said of **Walt Disney** that there were actually three Walts: the dreamer, the realist and the curmudgeon. You can take on various roles so that you can evaluate your creative project accord-ing to the "Walt Disney method": be the dreamer, the realist, the critic, and, as a complement, the neutral observer. They can help you look at what you are doing right now from the outside.

You can not only change your attitude/opinion in terms of perspective, but also your view of the creative process. What if you were to put everything that is "certain" into question? Can I eat cookies from a hovering cup? Are rubber boots only good for walking out in the rain? Can I only fill teapots with tea? Is fruit the only thing that can be stored in fruit crates? Who determines that? You can use every object, every situation, every cooking and baking recipe, and so on, for a different purpose and create something completely new for yourself out of it.

Dishware recycling: Here you can see a self-made étagère by **Herzallgaeuerliebst** (out of love for the Allgäu), a German blogger and artist from the Allgäu region, made from a set of dishes.

PRACTICE:
Test out the "Walt Disney method" on the basis of one of your current creative projects! If you wish, you can also try this out in a team with the roles given out.

You can make something new and individual out of old objects without much effort, by repurposing them and then allocating them a new form and function.

HERMIT OR TEAM PLAYER?

Whether you can be creative alone or in a team depends entirely on your own decision or preference—and probably on what kind of experience you have had so far. Depending on how large or small a project is in relation to the human resources (time expenditure, complexity of the tasks, financial expenditure and earnings, the own funds to be applied, such as materials, equipment, etc.), you will have to decide whether you want to do it alone or in a team. Being a hermit as well as working in a team both have advantages and disadvantages; you should be aware of them and make them part of your final decision.

Besides this, teamwork requires mutual trust. When you work in a team, you have to be willing to let go to a certain extent and to be able give up control. Everyone in the team should likewise be willing to compromise.

And teamwork takes time, especially for teams that have never worked together before. You should schedule this getting-to-know-you phase as part of the process. Once the team is well established, you will benefit greatly from it and save time and resources. Creativity will increase enormously because you will come up with more ideas together than if everyone were working on their own.

#HermitVsTeamplayer
#StrongTeam
#MarinaAbramović
#Ulay
#PerformanceArt
#Riptide
#Braunschweig
#AndréGiesler
#ChristianRank

Working Alone	Teamwork
+ No need for coordination with third parties	+ Bigger creative pool from which you can draw
+ Income doesn't have to be shared (so higher earnings)	+ Risk and responsibility are shared
	+ Lower time expenditure
– Smaller creative pool	+ Less personal contribution (such as initial financial payments)
– Risk and responsibility are yours alone	+ Potentially lower stress level
– You invest more time	
– Greater personal contribution (such as initial financial payments)	– Coordination with the team required; finding necessary compromise solutions
– Potentially higher level of stress	– Earnings will be shared
	– Potential for disagreements/disputes

Marina Abramović and **Ulay** are among the great pioneers of performance art. Their collaboration began in 1976. The artist couple, who also had a private relationship, developed pioneering performances that often got to the bottom of or even exceeded their physical limits. They parted in 1988 with a ninety-day performance on the Great Wall of China.

 *Do some of the practice exercises in this book by yourself and as part of a team. What do you notice? What are the differences (approaches, work processes, solutions)? Which do you prefer?*

Record shop, café, and art exhibition all in one: this is how the idea for the Café Riptide in Braunschweig, Germany came about. The team of André Ciesler and Christian Rank came up with the concept. These two friends and career-changers have received multiple awards for their creative teamwork.

THINGS DO HAPPEN BY CHANCE

Many ideas do not arise from something that was intentional, but simply by pure chance or happenstance. You are in the midst of the creative process and have an approximate goal in mind. Suddenly something unexpected happens, and your brush makes a blot, your wool for knitting or crocheting runs out too soon, or you mix up the quantities in a baking recipe, you don't have all the ingredients for something you are cooking and you just replace something with other ingredients. At home in my shared apartment, the latter is called "happenstance-pan cooking." These are moments (and the results that come out of them) that you initially rate negatively. In retrospect, however, some of this doesn't seem to be such a disaster and might even be better than what you originally intended!

Many innovations came about by chance, including penicillin, x-rays, Teflon coating, sticky notes, the telephone, photography, superglue, nylon stockings, and Velcro. And there is a name for this: all the positive discoveries, which were made by chance when someone had a different goal in mind, were made according to the "serendipity principle."

English musician **David Bowie** wrote most of his songs based this principle. He would take a text, such as one of his own or something from a newspaper, and break it down into individual words and sentences. Then he reassembled the snippets intuitively, like you would a puzzle. Bowie later used a computer program to do this.

So therefore, don't be afraid of nasty surprises! Something unforeseen can give you results that you couldn't have achieved on your own.

#SerendipityPrinciple
#Serendipity
#InnovationByChance
#DavidBowie
#Songwriting
#HelenGreen
#SplashOfColorPainting
#KatrinMerle
#HuskMitNavn
#3DPaperCraft

This Bowie illustration is by *Helen Green*.

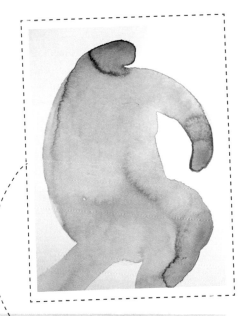

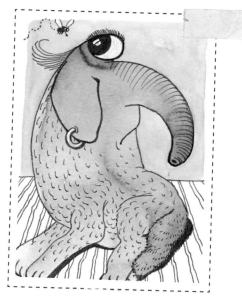

Illustrator **Katrin Merle** develops fantastic creatures from randomly painted, colored blots of india ink. She calls them "small doodle animals." The term "doodle" describes an aimless, oblivious, unconscious, and chance activity.

PRACTICE: *How can you incorporate chance into your creative process? Consciously think about such a course of action and try it out in your project! Do not be afraid of "mistakes"!*

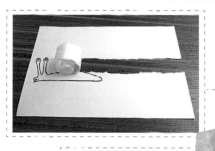

The pictures by Danish artist **Hus-kMitNavn** (Danish for "Remem-berMyName") seem like ironic comments on everyone's everyday problems. He uses a DIN A4 sheet of paper as the basis for creating an illustration, starting with a drawing in black and then manipulating it by tearing or folding the paper, which enhances the drawing content. Ultimately this creates a surprising 3-D effect.

HANG IN THERE; KEEP GOING!

Most ideas and projects fail because of a lack of motivation to move them forward and to finish them. Everyone knows that, and you certainly do. Sometimes your own failure is justified, and that is all right, but often it's simply due to a lack of staying power, too many distractions, a lack of priorities, letting your "inner Schweinehund"—your baser instincts—take over, or the eternal self-doubt that you just aren't good enough.

I can say from my own experience that creative work involves a lot of work and is exhausting! It's absolutely essential to motivate yourself, to be tenacious and persistent, and stick with it, as well as to continue working in a focused and disciplined way—both for the sake of your own creative work and the successful completion of a project. This is true even if, or when, you don't feel like doing it anymore; if you have meanwhile lost your courage in between and you have to accept setbacks or defeats. It can all be excruciating at times. It's therefore very important that you are able to praise yourself during these brief lows and thus are able to motivate yourself. Even though people often say that "praise in your own mouth stinks," I personally think it makes sense to praise yourself (especially when no one else does it) and to believe in what you are doing. Because you will also radiate this (or not).

A little trick when you think you can't go on, is to tell yourself: "I will now continue for . . . (something like ten minutes, a day, until I get to an intermediate step), and after that I have earned myself a break."

#Schweinehund
#Motivation
#SelfManagement
#FightYourWayThrough
#Tenacity
#Discipline
#StayingPower
#PraiseYourself
#AutoSuggestion
#RewardPrinciple

PRACTICE: *Keep on working based on the "reward principle" over a longer time, and test this method at a time when your motivation is low by saying the following:*

"When I have completed this task/dealt with this point on my list, then . . ." (please insert your personal reward here).

You will see that you will make progress (at least a bit, or a lot) this way!

"A PERSON SHOULD BY NO MEANS

APPEAR TO BE ANYTHING MORE

THAN HE OR SHE IS,

BUT NEITHER SHOULD

ANY PERSON PRAISE HERSELF

OR HIMSELF ANY LESS

THAN HE OR SHE IS WORTH."

JOACHIM PANTEN
(1947-2007)

AND NOW: TAKE A BREAK!

After you've been working hard, gotten a lot done, and gritted your teeth to get to your goal, now is the time to take a break! It certainly sounds pretty trivial at first, but that's exactly what many creative people often forget to do. At the same time, it's important that you consciously take some downtime and distance yourself from your creative work. On the one hand, you can recharge your own battery, and on the other hand, a break helps you to look at what you have achieved so far in a new way and from an external viewpoint. This way, you are able to assess just where you stand, what you can improve, and how things could go on, from a bit of distance and more objectively than before.

Aftera longer and conscious break, you'll get more new impulses, have different perspectives on the project and more energy to carry it out.

\#

\#TakingABreak
\#Relaxation
\#Mindfulness
\#Relax
\#PhysicalExerciseVsBeingLazy
\#LeisureTime
\#ShortVacation
\#GetMyHeadClear
\#Recharge

PRACTICE: 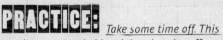 *Take some time off. This can be an extended lunch break, a day off, or a (short) vacation. Just the time that you need and can spare. Anything that lets you relax, take a break and recharge your batteries, get some exercise, visit a museum, go to the seaside, etc. Try to switch off during this time and completely forget about your creative project.*

PRESCRIPTION №21

SPARRING PARTNER

Am I boxing here? No, of course not. Nevertheless, you can "spar" with something or someone in the creative area. This is a good way to try out future situations and/or test your creative output before things actually get "serious." It's important that you choose a suitable sparring partner. She or he should be working on a level equal to yours or be an appropriate match for the future consumers of your project. With your partner, you will be putting yourself in a practice situation in which you can test everything you are not yet sure about, whether it will work, or test whether people will comprehend your project and your ideas properly. It's likely that you will encounter weak points in the process, but that is exactly the goal of sparring. Your sparring partner is a kind of mirror from whom you can get a reading, who gives you feedback on your project, and with whom you go through everything once. He or she should be a good match for the situation, and be neutral, impartial, discreet, and honest. In a company, it's a person such as a coach, moderator, or mentor who takes on this role. Like boxing, creative sparring is a protected situation, which means you are not taking any kind of risks. After you spar, it's a matter of gathering up insights and impulses that improve your idea and your concept or push it in a new direction. As part of the creative process, you should latch on to the practice of sparring during the last third of your project. If necessary, you can hold several sparring sessions (for more complex projects), such as after each phase of the project. Small tip: A peer group* can also be your sparring partner!

#
#Boxing
#Duel
#SparringSession
#TrainingIsImportant
#PracticeSituation
#TestRun
#Improvement
#Optimization
#PeerGroup
#JulianeWenzl
#UtagawaKuniyoshi
#Sumo

**PRACTICE:** *Who could be a sparring partner for your project?*
Towards the end of the creative phase, test out your project with a friend or colleague. A group of like-minded people (peer group) is also a possibility.

*A peer group is a group of people with common interests, with comparable origins, of similar age, or of the same social status, and a mutual relationship is present between the individual and the group.

Boxing is one of the subjects that illustrator **Jullane Wenzl** deals with. Whether her drawings are about sparring or actual fights is not known.

There is also sparring in the ring during Japanese sumo wrestling, as there is in most one-on-one sports. The above picture is an ink drawing by **Utagawa Kuniyoshi**.

BE INTERDISCIPLINARY

To enhance your creativity, it can be helpful and make sense to go beyond your own boundaries. This doesn't necessarily mean leaving your own comfort zone, but rather leaving your field of activity and area of competence. But don't worry, you don't have to be on your own in the new environment. You can seek out an expert, someone who is at home in this field, for help. Together you can enrich your respective specialist knowledge and get a project going; a project that neither of you would have been able to accomplish by yourself. Imagine the projects that could come about when a designer and an architect work together, or a musician and a painter, or a mathematician and a copywriter, or a fashion designer and a chemist. Completely new and very innovative projects can be created based on this interdisciplinary approach.

Another possibility would be for you to look into areas outside your own field and observe how people work there. What would be their approach to posing a problem, and which materials and processes do they use, for what reasons? Can you transfer some of this into your creative process, something that didn't exist in your sector before?

Prescription No. 21 dealt with the theme of "sparring partners." Imagine an interdisciplinary sparring model: your sparring partner would be part of a different sector than you are. By using this form of collegial advice, this would likewise result in a great boost in creativity on both sides!

# #

#Interdisciplinary
#ComfortZone
#AreaofCompetence
#CollegialAdvice
#TravelGuidebook
ForAnimals
#IngaMarieRamcke
#ToniaWiatrowski
#HellaJongerius
#IKEA
#UNICEF
#Cooperation
#WallHanging
#HelpProgram

PRACTICE: *Think and act in an interdisciplinary way. What would that look like for your project? To do this, take a non-creative sector, such as information technology, chemistry, or environmental technology. Talk to an expert in this sector and share your experiences and knowledge with one another.*

Inga Marie Ramcke, a doctoral candidate in the didactics of biology, and illustrator Tonia Wiatrowski worked as a team to come up with the idea for the world's first "travel guidebook for animals." The resulting children's non-fiction book accompanies twenty-five animals on their trips around the world and along the way also explains the behavior of draft animals. Here, the competencies of the pair of authors complemented each other in an interdisciplinary way. However, except for coming to the joint idea for the book, there was a strict division of labor: Inga did the research and wrote the texts; Tonia took on designing and illustrating the book.

Dutch product designer Hella Jongerius developed three wall hangings in cooperation with the Swedish furniture chain IKEA®, which were manufactured in India in cooperation with the aid organization UNICEF. In this way, all three cooperating partners supported the program, which enabled Indian women to set up a small sewing company and thereby earn school fees for their children.

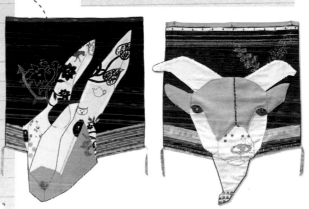

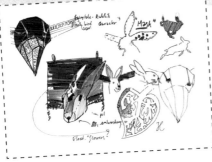

TAKE THE ELEVATOR

Imagine that you are already right in the middle of your project in conceptual terms. It's going well and you are about to finish it successfully. The only thing you still need is someone to support your new project (such as by publication, financial support, production, sales). Imagine further that you are in an elevator and, suddenly, exactly the person who could promote your project and thus advance it steps into the elevator. You gather up all your courage and speak to this—for you—very important person. You have about thirty seconds before you have to get out. How do you present your project in a few key sentences? What are the features, what are the advantages of your project? Are you excited? Can you find the right words? What is your effect on your counterpart? Do you have the power of persuasion?

This thought experiment, which can very easily become a reality in your everyday work (maybe not necessarily in an elevator, but at other events such as network meetings, couses, trade fairs, specialist conferences, etc.), is called an "elevator pitch" or "elevator statement." It's a method you can use to rehearse for situations like this. Real and spontaneous sales pitches are not easy to make because you have to be able to act on several levels at the same time.

The more you practice making an "elevator pitch," the better at it and therefore the more relaxed you will become. Another advantage is that being able to formulate and say out loud what you are currently working on and what gets you "fired up" allows you to work towards the goal in a more focused way, and this can thus lead to enhancing your creativity.

# #

#ElevatorPitch
#ElevatorStatement
#60Seconds
#RidingAnElevator
#Networking
#BeingBrave

PRACTICE: *Practice your elevator pitch by asking a colleague or friend to play the potential sponsor. Try to be brief (no more than a minute) and pay close attention to your choice of words and your expressions. Afterwards, interview your test person about how he or she perceived you and what was said! (Was what was said understandable? Did it have a positive impact? What was his or her overall impression of you and the project?)*

1. **Find the right moment** (a feel for the situation).
2. **Get the statement across in three to five sentences,** paying attention to:
   - your body language & rhetoric (choice of words, emphasis, pauses);
   - clear, unambiguous language (understandable, interesting);
   - addressing and emphasizing the advantages for your counterpart;
   - positive overall impression & composure (neither excited nor arrogant; communicate at eye level).
3. **Say goodbye with a "sender address"**
   - a business card, or say, "I'll send you a short message" or something similar.

Checklist

PRACTICE, PRACTICE, PRACTICE

There is a short joke about the following prescription, which goes something like this: A man is looking for Carnegie Hall in New York City and asks a passerby: "Excuse me, how do I get to Carnegie Hall?" "You have to practice, practice, practice!" I often think of this joke when it comes to the issue of "practice makes perfect." There is a lot of truth to both the joke and the saying. Of course, creative achievement requires talent, maybe a bit of luck and chance, but without the effort and the will to constantly improve yourself, to learn new things, paired with a serving of persistence and perseverance, you will not be able to consistently improve your creativity.

Painter and sculptor **Alberto Giacometti** is an example of trying things out, repeating, and practicing for his entire life, but also despairing and doubting his own creative work. He said of himself, "It's true that I am rarely satisfied. In fact, that's why I keep on working." And so he kept drawing the same subject (i.e., people) over and over again. He produced an infinite amount of material, half of which he immediately destroyed because it was not good enough for him. "If I could only succeed in drawing or painting or modeling something, it wouldn't be so bad. If only one head, one head, would work out for me, just once." For all that, or precisely because of this, Giacometti's works are among the best known and most important of the twentieth century.

But so much agonizing self-doubt is by no means necessary! On the contrary, my tip is that successful practice—which will build up over time—will motivate you to continue your creative work. See you at Carnegie Hall!

#

#AlbertoGiacometti
#Selfdoubt
#Longtermproject
#Repetition
#WilhelmKoch
#Cheesesandwiches
#MichelGondry
#1000portraits

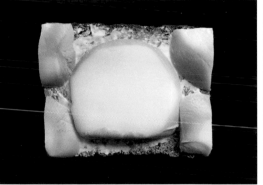

Wilhelm Koch has a very special long-term photographic project: he eats a cheese sandwich every day. Before he eats it, however, he makes a ritual of photographing every piece of bread artfully topped with cheese. In the meantime, Koch has collected thousands of photos and perfected his photographic style.

PRACTICE: *Long-term projects give you a good chance to optimize your skills. This will keep you on the ball, make your creative idea more profound and play through it over and over again. Repetition is practice!*

Find a long-term project In your preferred discipline and think about the intervals when you would like to work on it. Then the word is: keep it up!

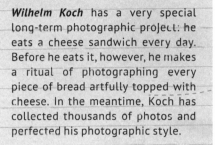

On his website, French filmmaker **Michel Gondry** called on fans to send him a portrait photograph. For a fee of $20, he would make a drawing from them and then send you the original. As a result of his diligent work, he also created the publication *1000 Portraits*.

TELL STORIES

Many areas of creative work are based on telling stories, be it a story wrapped in a song or a music video; in a movie, a book, a board game; in role playing or a video game; on a website; in a play, a comic book, an opera, or a dance; and so forth. Even in advertising, stories are told every day in order to sell products. Because people just love stories!

When you start a creative project, you can think beforehand about what story you want to tell with it. Do you want to share something personal with your target audience? What is behind your creative drive? Which stories impel you forward? Although or precisely because our society is becoming a more and more lonely one, there is a growing number of vloggers and bloggers who tell stories about their everyday lives from home and thus generate many virtual followers.

Each medium has tools and rules for storytelling. Take a look at how others are doing it in their respective sector, and then find your own individual way, your "language," and your style for telling stories. Authenticity is just as important as "that certain something" for you to get be noticed at all in all the media oversupply. And that applies to every creative sector. You may have the feeling that every story has already been told—and that is probably true! But it hasn't been told yet from your (creative) perspective!

#CreativeSectors
#Storytelling
#DriveForAction
#Vlogger
#Blogger
#Follower
#Authenticity
#ThatCertainSomething
#YourPerspective
#StoryByChance
#FrankWedekind
#FrühlingsErwachen
#SpringAwakening
#DuncanSheik
#StevenSater
#Broadway
#IGSFranzschesFeld
#FranzvonStuck
#kunstanstifterverlag
#RobertaBergmann

PRACTICE: *Write a story by chance! To do this, use the snippet technique described on page 46. You can cut out random words or pictures (such as from a magazine), reassemble them, and then develop a story from them. As a variation, you can write the story as a drama, a love story and as a mystery story.*

In 1891, *Frank Wedekind* wrote the children's tragedy *Frühlings Erwachen* (*Spring Awakening*). In it, he tells of the struggle in growing up. In this story, Wedekind denounces the prudery and hypocrisy of society. Not only did it create a huge scandal back then and was censored for a long time, and even banned in the original version; the story is still controversial today. For example, in 2009, there was a mother in Switzerland who accused her child's teacher of "distributing pornographic material to minors" because he discussed this book in German class. Today it's one of the most frequently performed dramas worldwide and is also once again part of the curriculum in many schools. Besides various productions for the theater, there is also a successful musical adaptation by *Steven Sater* (book and lyrics) and *Duncan Sheik* (music). Starting in 2006, it was performed at the *Eugene O'Neill Theater* on Broadway as *Spring Awakening*. In 2018, I saw the German adaptation of the musical in the production by the *Integrierten Gesamtschule (integrated comprehensive school) Franzsches Feld* in Braunschweig, Germany, and documented it as a photographer. But not only theatrical performers are inspired by it. As early as 1891, *Franz von Stuck* drew the cover of the first edition according to Wedekind's specifications.

In 2014, the original text was published as an anniversary edition (for Wedekind's 150th birthday anniversary), illustrated for the first time, by *kunstanstifter verlag* ("art instigator" publisher) —with my illustrations!

NO DOGMATISM, PLEASE!

"Don't be so damn dogmatic now!" You may have heard this statement about the way you work. At the same time, you only wanted to stick to the rules of the game. In common parlance, dogmatism is associated with narrow-mindedness and has a negative connotation. Knowing the basic "rules of the game" for your field of work is important and, in my opinion, indispensable. Because only if you know the rules can you consciously *flout them*. You don't need to dogmatically adhere to the rules of the game in every situation. Sometimes disregarding the rules is what is really appealing. Breaking them on purpose and consciously is a creative method that you can use for yourself and your creative work, such as to stimulate your lateral and divergent thinking and way of acting *(see page 11)*.

Many pioneers, trailblazers, and creative people act on the principle of following as many guidelines, basic knowledge, "how-to-dos," and principles as necessary (this also has something to do with experience and professionalism), but also as few as possible, so that you don't restrict yourself too much and continue to give a free rein to creative action. Creative careers and successes seldom emerge on the drawing board; thus, they aren't part of a larger plan that has to follow certain rules of the game in order for them to work (as may be the case in other professions). Hence my tip: have the courage to break the rules if it makes sense for your creative work.

#

#RulesOfTheGame
#Dogma
#LateralThinking
#DivergentThinking
#Trailblazer
#Courage
#BreakTheRules
#Authenticity
#MontyPython
#Comedy
#TheFourthWall
#FrankZappa
#Virtuoso

PRACTICE: *You are working on your project right now (see, for example, the practice on page 31). Think about how you can break the given rules (from the client; or those set up by yourself, etc.) or, if that isn't possible, at least interpret them more broadly. What does this change in your way of thinking and acting?*

Pictorial comparison: if you always cook a certain dish according to a recipe—what happens if once time you improvise or interpret it freely instead?

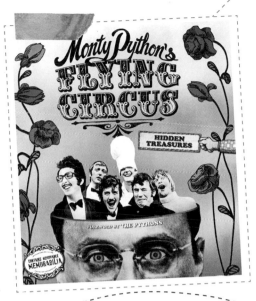

British comedy group **Monty Python** is known as a rule-breaker and thus as a groundbreaker in terms of both form and content. The six comedians were the first to create absurd, skits which did not have any point at all; this initially irritated the audience but became a style-defining trademark for the group. They succeeded in revolutionizing the comedy genre through their unconventional narrative style, by inserting breaks and by using elaborately, drawn animated sequences. Due to the way they performed, they often broke through "the fourth wall" (i.e., the imaginary wall of a theater stage, the side open to the audience where the players do not act, and that is not crossed) by communicating directly with the audience.

American musician and composer **Frank Zappa** significantly shaped the musical world with over one hundred music albums. Today he is considered a style icon of rock music. His textual and compositional style did not follow the usual rules for rock 'n' roll, but rather went way beyond them. Zappa experimented in his music, was excessive, often socially critical, and humorous, with borrowings from Dadaist-absurdism, and was open to many genres. He mixed these various influences wildly in a kind of collage style. He also created many orchestral works and a lot of film music. Besides all this, Frank Zappa was considered a virtuoso electric guitarist, among other things because he used to play his instrument differently from anyone else. In his playing, a solo could last ten minutes (that's five to ten times longer than guitar solos usually take), and he was one of the few to play all positions of the fingerboard.

Christophe Delbrouck

FRANK ZAPPA
& les mères de l'invention

Le Castor Astral

EXPERIMENT

Philosopher **Friedrich Wilhelm Nietzsche** said: "In truth, wanting something means doing an experiment to find out what we can do." I think there is nothing more liberating than just experimenting without having a specific goal in mind. The way should be the goal when experimenting. It's important to find out what you can do and what suits you (or not), what new things you are discovering, and what can lead to innovation in your work. An experiment should give you new impulses or reveal something new to you, something that you would never have come up with in theory or by using your usual approach. Experimentation always means a trial-and-error principle; the risk of failure isn't a small one. But the chances are also greater that you will encounter something new and surprising, and this will enhance your creativity because you are treading unknown pathways. Mistakes are also not something bad; rather, they can help you to optimize your pathway and to improve your approach. Don't be afraid to be wrong! I often calm myself down by saying that everyone makes mistakes and that this is part of being human and learning. It makes you stronger and moves you forward. I know from my experience that experiments almost always produce results that help me on personally. Therefore, I find it important to deliberately plunge into the unknown every now and then and try out things that you've never done before; you don't know exactly how and whether such things will work. But you are curious enough to find out exactly that. The result of the experiment is often completely different than expected—not necessarily worse, but simply more surprising.

\#
#TheWayIsTheGoal
#NewImpulses
#TrialAndError
#TetraPakEtching
#Etching
#Upcycling
#DIYMusicalInstruments
#Smarticular

PRACTICE: *Take a look at your trash: what do you find in it that can still be creatively reused and upcycled for your projects? Experiment with these unusual materials (such as musical instruments, stamps/ printing techniques, decorative objects, flower pots, flower vases, mobiles, sewing, pictures/ collages, snippet technique, wrapping paper, cooking leftovers).*

I attended a printmaking workshop. There, instead of the usual etching plates of metal (such as steel or zinc), cut-open Tetra Pak® milk or juice packs were used. We then rubbed black ink into the etchings created this way and printed.

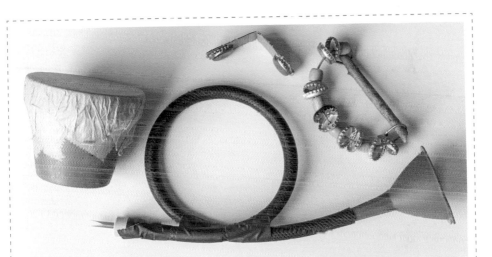

The *smarticular.net* blog shows how you can make functional musical instruments from normal household items. You can use a bottle cap, for example, to make castanets and a tambourine; a flowerpot and some baking paper become a drum; and a garden hose, funnel, wine cork, and straw can be made into a trumpet using some tape.

BROADENING YOUR HORIZONS

Your creativity feeds on your experiences and your knowledge of everything possible. Quenching your thirst for knowledge, going on a journey of discovery, learning something new every day—all form your creative personality and allow it to grow.

People strive for security and stability, but that generally stands in the way of a creative drive for action and innovation. Change is a catalyst for creativity. It's necessary to be able to be creative every day anew and to do this again and again from a different perspective. All that you need to do is to be willing to take a few risks and be curious, and you shouldn't be afraid to step out of your comfort zone. When you are ready for all of this, you can learn new things and make them your own.

My tip: try to broaden your horizons as often as you can! Take a class at a community college or do an online tutorial. Go on a trip (be it a vacation or an educational trip), sometimes work in a different place, look at a lot of things (books, films, theater, conferences, festivals, exhibitions, musical events). Break through your everyday life and the daily routine (do things differently than usual, make things more varied). Create an inspiring balance of leisure time, something that will restore your creative energy. Get to know new people, meet like-minded people, exchange ideas with one another—networking is always a good way to get feedback, criticism, and confirmation. See how others do things (and learn from it).

\#
#ThirstForKnowledge
#JourneyOfDiscovery
#DriveForAction
#Innovation
#Change
#WillingToTakeRisks
#Curiosity
#ComfortZone
#Wanderlust
#ChangeOfPlace
#BookBindingCourse
#MarieDann
#IslandExperience

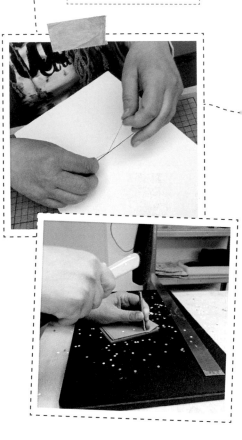

"We run up against it, feel it, and move in time. Everyone takes their time here. A year. A bicycle. And a little courage. And rides off. I am that someone." With these words, designer and artist **Marie Dann** describes her project. *Iceland Year* was her project that was meant to see the horizon with different eyes, to "broaden" it. She financed this independent project through a Crowdfunding campaign via the **Startnext** platform and by promising supporters that the results of the project would include a limited-edition hand-bound book. When Marie then came back to Germany, she got to work, designed and published a more-than-400-page photo diary of her trip.

I give bookbinding courses for adults. It strikes me every time how little the participants trust themselves at the beginning of the course, but how curious they are nonetheless. At the end of the course, everyone is very proud of their little book objects and almost can't believe they made them by themselves.

PRACTICE:

Ask yourself: What else would I like to learn (in life, in work) that I haven't tried yet or have postponed until later? Make up your mind to learn it, register for a course, for example, and then just go through with it! Consciously take the time to do this and see what happens.

IMPROVISE

To improvise means "to do something freely and spontaneously on purpose." And you can practice improvising! In the beginning, it might feel strange, and perhaps you are insecure, a little anxious, or tense. But if you dare and have a little courage, just do it, preferably without turning everything over in your head too much. Improvising can help you in many life situations. Improvising is the ability to let go, to adjust to a situation spontaneously and not to control it; to let yourself be carried away by the moment and not to stop yourself under any circumstances (although you don't know what is happening), but to stay in the "flow," trusting that it will continue and that something fruitful will develop out of this spontaneity.

Improvisation is possible in all areas of life, whether in private everyday life or at work. When creative people improvise, they usually go consciously—but also unconsciously—on a journey of discovery. And their own artistic areas can even emerge from this. In music, for example, people generally know about "jam sessions" where all the musicians involved improvise together; in jazz this is called "free jazz"; in drama there is the sub-form called "improvisational theater." If texts are recited or rapped spontaneously, this is called "freestyle"; in modern dance, there is "contact improvisation," when participants dance in a mindful way but without intent (and choreography), in order to explore all of the body's potential for movement.

All the examples mentioned use improvisation to develop independent and free works. Works that perhaps may only be seen or heard one time.

#

#Impromptu
#FreeJazz
#IntuitiveMusic
#JamSession
#ImproTheater
#Freestyle
#ContactImprovisation
#JetztUndHier
#Podcast
#ComedyImpro
#GuteArbeitOriginals

PRACTICE:

Finish off a creative task (from your preferred area) in that you just go ahead and do it. To complete this task, it's forbidden to plan, to proceed according to a usual pattern/recipe, or to know the solution or the exact goal in advance. If you are getting nowhere, improvise! Don't let yourself be unsettled, just always keep going!

At the independent improvisational theater group, *Jetzt und Hier (Here and Now)*, the audience is included in the theatrical performance. The audience calls out various terms for the performers, which are then incorporated into the spontaneous play, much to the delight of the audience. The actors have almost no props or costumes available for their use. The actors' performance is accompanied by spontaneous music and is a unique experience every evening.

The improvisation podcast *Gute Arbeit Impro*, which is well worth listening to, by the comedy group *Gute Arbeit Originals (Good Work Originals)* runs for around twenty to thirty minutes per audio episode and is recorded in a completely improvised way by the actors involved. On the basis of three given terms, they create various skits and comic scenes through dialogue.

KEEP IT SIMPLE!

I'm sure you know the saying, "The simplest ideas are usually the best!" Nevertheless, the simplest ideas are often the most difficult ones because simplicity is not that easy. It takes courage to omit (and to discard) things, to reduce them, to make ideas precise, to communicate clearly, and to be "ingenious" in terms of content. This thought often puts me under pressure. Then I say to myself: "Don't panic! I don't have to be a genius on command!" Rather, I think about how my idea can be broken down to the essentials and concentrated to communicate it in the best way possible.

This method of reduction and simplicity is used to write haikus, headlines, short messages, or *Twitter*. Each tweet can only be a maximum of 280 Unicode characters.

You can easily transfer the method to your personal, creative area or your project. You can cook something delicious with just a few ingredients. You can come up with great pictures using just one technique (such as photography, printmaking, painting, drawing, or film). Your music can sound very good using just *one* musical instrument or a *single* melody. A piece of clothing doesn't have to be made in a complicated cut using many individual parts; think of simple solutions such as a short skirt or a poncho. Or if you're designing jewelry, a chain or ring doesn't always have to be ostentatious (and thus possibly give the impression of "overload"). By reducing the piece to a few shapes and materials, you can convey minimalism and a high-quality, clear aesthetic.

# #

#SimpleIdeas
#Reduction
#Precision
#Twitter
#Cooking
#Photography
#PrintGraphics
#Painting
#Drawing
#Sewing
#JeweleryDesign
#Minimalism
#Aesthetics
#TinkeringSchool
#DavidShrigley

The American initiative **Tinkering School** offers workshops and summer camps for children and young people where they can make functional products based on various themes on their own. The participants get an introduction in all the workshops as well as tools, and then use them themselves under the guidance of adults! In this way, they make soap boxes, treehouses, and boats from the simplest of materials (such as wood, trash, screws, and broken everyday objects).

PRACTICE:

Attempt to simplify one of your ideas based on the "Keep it simple" idea! Shorten, reduce, and compress things as radically as you can. In the process, go beyond your boundaries. What do you really need in terms of technique and material? What can you do without? What content can you delete without replacing it?
Then, check whether the reduction improved your idea or not.

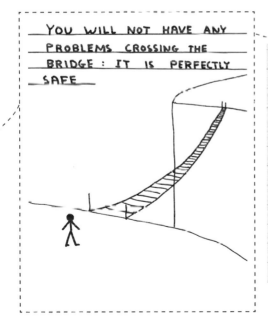

YOU WILL NOT HAVE ANY PROBLEMS CROSSING THE BRIDGE : IT IS PERFECTLY SAFE

British artist **David Shrigley** is famous for his black-and-white cartoons, which fill many books and are widely published. He is often accused of almost not being able to draw because his drawing style features a simple and uncertain, non-naturalistic line. In the texts he often attaches, he likes to leave spelling mistakes or strikethroughs; they are part of the content and black-humor comedy. Shrigley's cartoons have a deliberately unfinished effect on the viewer. Their visual impact is very clear, reduced and very precise on the linguistic level, hitting the core of the matter.

INTUITION OR THE FIRST IDEA

If you turn back to Prescription Nº. 3 (see page 34) again, which involved finding ideas (finding a theme), I would now like to remind you of this starting situation and the potential for catharsis (Greek *kátharsis* = cleansing, in the sense of a spontaneous creating by drawing from within yourself). What was the first idea that crossed your mind while you were thinking things over?

With *Prescription Nº. 31*, I appeal to your intuition: trust and believe in your very first ideas! From my own experience, I can say that your first ideas take on great significance. Again and again, I intuitively—and mostly unconsciously—come back to my initial ideas.

When I am teaching, I like to assign tasks that have to be completed within a short period of time. This way, the participants don't have all that much time to plan or think about it. One of the practices, I have developed together with a colleague, is to visualize terms using only a certain number of wooden sticks of different lengths and a pot of glue. Within an hour, a three-dimensional object made of wood is created.

Designer **Nina Sieverding** developed the font "**Ding Siever**" in an impromptu typography practice exercise during her basic undergraduate studies. The font name was an allusion to her last name and the already existing Ding fonts. Nina's first idea was to develop a font from a modular point system. In the end, she simply tried it out by sticking removable black adhesive dots on walls and floors in an experimental way. This way, she could quickly and easily test the effect of the font from a distance.

PRACTICE: *Take a morning to practice catharsis or spontaneous creation by drawing from within yourself. Don't expect anything; just play around with materials and tools. As you do this, take note of your thoughts and ideas and, if necessary, write down your first ideas without evaluating or criticizing them.*
On another day, take another look at what you wrote down and try to develop something concrete from these ideas.

SELECTIVE PERCEPTION

"The brain filters and shows us the world as it suits us." If you deal with a theme over a longer time, your perception changes about the things that surround you and that you encounter daily. This psychological phenomenon, also known as "selective perception," occurs because your brain is constantly searching for connections and patterns. At the same time, some aspects of your environment will be filtered, sharpened, and highlighted based on your theme. They catch your eye. The opposite is also true: certain aspects will become suppressed and seem to fade into the background. You are constantly exposed to an abundance of stimuli in everyday life. Through selective perception, you can channel this overstimulation to be able to focus yourself on certain impressions and stimuli. But take care: selective perception can also tempt you to overlook important information! Some scientists call this a serious defect or attention blindness of the brain. I believe that selective perception has something more of a positive influence on your creative work! You can gather and archive further relevant impressions and later summon them up from a much larger pool of information and use them for your creative work. What do you have to do to perceive selectively? Nothing! Because that happens automatically anyway. As a tip: remain open, unbiased, critical, and vigilant.

#
#SelectivePerception
#Psychology
#BrainResearch
#Subconscious
#Overstimulation
#Mindfulness
#ResearchPhase
#Pareidolia
#FabianNilius

PRACTICE: *Review your selective perception based on a subject that interests you or that you are currently working on. Look at something (with your theme in mind) that has absolutely nothing to do with your theme. That might be a book, a magazine, social media, a website, a movie, music, or something similar (anything that provides you with input). Can you still find information related to your subject that lends itself to being linked to your theme? Can you use any of this for your creative work?*

Perhaps you know this already: you are looking at an object for a long time and suddenly you discover a face within its form, or you suddenly perceive the object itself as if it were a living thing.

This visual phenomenon is called "pareidolia" (ancient Greek: *poro* = beside, *eidolon* = form, appearance).

German photographer *Fabian Nilius* created the portraits of the characters shown here.

"Did you know that the the brain automatically ignores unnecessary information? Just like the second 'the' in the previous sentence."

VISUALIZE IDEAS

Thinking through your ideas in theory is one thing; putting them into practice and visualizing them is completely different (and the next step). The process of visual thinking, such as sketching, is significantly more complex and concrete. You can really find out whether an idea is really worth its salt only when you try to visualize it for yourself and for others and thus formulate it.

Making your creative idea visible will not only help you gain clarity about what you want to achieve with it. It will also help others understand it (and you) better. For example, if you just talk about an idea, then everyone has a different image in her or his mind's eye.

When you sketch something, you are thinking with the pencil on paper. When you cook something spontaneously, you are thinking with the ingredients, spices, and kitchen utensils that are available to you at that moment. When you design furniture, you are thinking with the materials and tools that you use. No matter what you are working on creatively, when it's transferred from your head to reality for the first time, the idea takes on a different quality.

That's why it's important to try to visualize all the ideas that are important to you in the quickest way possible. Find your own visual language, try it out, and see it as an opportunity to test, further develop, and improve your idea.

#VisualThinking
#Sketching
#VisualLanguage
#123Ideas
#IdeasAndThoughts
#HelmutSmits
#Humorous

PRACTICE: *Transfer one of your ideas (which previously has only existed in your head) into visual reality. To do this, use such things as a storyboard, a mind map, a vision board, a mood board, an infographic, an illustration, or a sketch. Then show the result to a counterpart and discuss what is visualized.*

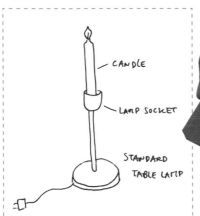

CANDLE

LAMP SOCKET

STANDARD
TABLE LAMP

As an international visual artist, **Helmut Smits** incessantly produces new artistic ideas, which he visualizes in advance using small black-and-white sketches. He published some of these idea sketches in two short books (*123 Ideas*, *Ideas and Thoughts*). His works often appear to the viewer as humorous, conceptual comments on his personal view of our contemporary (consumer) society.

"Iron pattern": when you declare your ironing mishap to be intentional. "Bookend": If you don't have any bookends, but you don't want the books to fall over, take one of the books from the shelf, stick it under the bookshelves, and you don't need bookends for the rest of the books!

ROLE MODELS & GUIDING FIGURES

A role model can inspire you to fully exploit your creative potential. American sociologist **Robert K. Merton** defines "role models" as people whose lives serve as examples for others and who are seen as guiding figures. They can be people from your own social environment, such as a teacher, parents, siblings, friends, sports trainers, peers, colleagues, or politically, socially, creatively, or culturally committed people. It doesn't have to be a famous personality or perfect-looking role model (nobody is perfect)!

Having role models can inspire you creatively! You can use your role model to motivate yourself to achieve your goals more consistently! But this does not involve becoming a copy of your role model. You are you; you have your own qualities and strengths, and you may even be a role model for someone else! Your hero may perhaps not be a real, existing person at all, but rather an (idealized) version of yourself, a dream and ideal image or a future version of yourself?

#RoleModel
#RobertK.Merton
#Companion
#Sponsor
#RoleModels
#GuidingFigures
#OttoErnst
#Questionnaire

A little piece of advice from the German writer **Otto Ernst**, about not regarding the "role models and guiding figures" method as a panacea:

Following role models is good, but it's only the ideal that we find ourselves that gives our actions a living nerve.

Otto Ernst

PRACTICE:

If you feel like using the "role models and guiding figures" method for yourself to enhance your creativity, then ask yourself in a quiet moment:

1) Who are the heroes of your childhood?

2) Who are your role models for what you do professionally or creatively?

3) Why do you admire this/these person(s)? What makes them different from you in your eyes—and is it really so (seen objectively, without your fan glasses)?

4) Where exactly do the differences between yourself and your guiding figure lie? Do you have an influence on this; that is, can you approach your role model? If yes, how?

5) Where does your own potential lie? How can you increase it and, finally, take full advantage of it (with regard to your future self)?

RESEARCH SPIRIT & INVENTIVE SPIRIT

A researcher finds herself or himself in a permanent learning process and in a systematically planned experimental phase in which he or she seeks answers to his or her questions. They are trying to find out something that no one has discovered before! The inventor creates by drawing from within themselves and thinks up things that are new and, in their opinion, necessary to improve social life or to enrich it in some way.

This inner drive that researchers and inventors sense is something that people who are creative can also acquire. In general, creative people also demonstrate this behavior. They are eager to learn and acquire knowledge; they often experiment in the work they do; they look for answers (because there is a problem or a question to be solved); they draw from within themselves to be creative and in the process develop new works that didn't exist before and which are able to improve the lives of those who benefit from them (music fans, bookworms, art lovers, dance lovers, et al.), if not actually even change those lives in the best case.

My tip: sometimes see yourself (even) more as a researcher and inventor in the work you are doing! Because you might be doing pioneering work in your field. This, incidentally, also makes you an expert! In creative work, the way is often just as important as the goal, and it's not always easy to find new pathways. You have to fight against prevailing opinions and perhaps have to first convince the beneficiaries of your creative output about yourself or your idea.

#
#Learn
#Research
#Invent
#InnerDrive
#CreativeExpert
#PersuasiveWork
#LionelPalm
#GeraldDissen
#RoomInABox
#SebastianThies
#Nat-2

PRACTICE: *Think about how you can use innovation and an inventive spirit to design something in your creative field—something that did not exist before—and thus improve or enrich social life. You can also take up something that already exists and consider how it can be improved.*

Most furniture is heavy and immobile. The two managing directors of **Room in a Box, Gerald Dissen** and **Lionel Palm**, wanted to change that! With an inventive spirit, they developed a range of cardboard furniture that can be easily assembled and disassembled in just a few minutes. And if you don't need it, you can fold the furniture up to save space and move it aside! This made-in-Germany furniture, made from sustainable corrugated cardboard, generates low emissions on the one hand and is durable on the other. A cardboard bed is not a temporary solution, but rather a full-fledged alternative to a conventional metal or wooden bed. And cardboard furniture is not only comfortable, it also looks pretty good, has a regulating effect on the room climate, and is affordable.

Businessman **Sebastian Thies** invents and produces unusual sneakers as part of his **"nat-2"** label, founded in 2007. The label experiments with the widest range of materials, some of which had not previously been used for making shoes. These include braided aluminum or varnished cork in various color shades, and the shoes feature 3-D optics and materials that change their color according to the temperature. Together with his father, Thies also developed convertible shoes that can be transformed in a few seconds from sneakers to sandals and from sandals to ankle-high sneakers or boots. So you get a two-in-one or four-in-one shoe, depending on the style, which you can also recombine using styles from the series in different colors.

HUMOR

Having a sense of humor and understanding it requires a certain open attitude about life. Those who want to be seen as taking themselves seriously (the German expression is people who "go to the cellar to laugh") are not exactly open to life.

To be humorous in your own creative work if the theme allows it (such as by using irony, satire, a double meaning, something tongue in cheek) requires that you deal with the subject intelligently and can think laterally. You should be able, when telling a joke or a punch line, to make something abstract and put it in a nut-shell.

Humor is very much linked to your own creativity, whether you can laugh at yourself, whether you allow others to laugh with you, or whether you consciously make others laugh and think by what you are doing. You can improve your creative work and improve its quality through humor. Humor can be used like a creative method. With a pinch of humor, you can make complex content clearer or spice up dry content. Humor can be a key to addressing and reaching people directly. Most of them would rather be happy than serious or sad. Humor is positive and usually brings us closer together. In many creative areas, humor is an important stylistic device, such as in advertising.

With humor, you can be critical in a more subtle and entertaining way than without it, such as by using sarcasm, ridicule, irony, and satire.

# #

#Openness
#Joke
#Sarcasm
#Irony
#Satire
#LateralThinking
#Abstraction
#StylisticDevice
#VorWerbeagentur
#DieWeltBereichertDresden
#Politikaward2015
#JakobWessinger
#YuanPeng
#WessingerUndPeng

Wordplay in a poster thought up by **VOR Werbeagentur** (advertising agency) for the Die-Welt-bereichert-Dresden ("The world enriches Dresden") campaign which was awarded the "Politikaward" ("Politics Award") in 2015.

Wessinger und Peng

Konzeption Gestaltung Redaktion Alle Kunden W&P World

Rainer Brenner
AMG

Museum für Naturkunde
Website Naturdetektive

Theodor Heuss Stiftung
Jubiläumszeitung

Publicitas
Cinema Trends & Insights

Junge Freunde Staatsgalerie
Corporate Design

Deutscher Apotheker Verlag
MMP

Triest Verlag
Corporate Design

Deutscher Apotheker Verlag
Chance Pharmazie

DAV Mediengruppe
Corporate Design

Yves Suter
Motorrer

Spielplatz Zeitung
Ausgabe N° 1

Optkooch
Einfach Sehen

← 1 2 3 →

Jakob Wessinger and Yuan Peng's German–Swiss agency, *Wessinger und Peng*, which they founded in 2008, would definitely not be the same without the use of irony and humor. Their trademark is being tongue in cheek; their visual signboard is a wink. Whether by means of publications such as *wagazin and puch–Das Alphabet* or their Facebook posts on the subject of "connections," Wessinger and Peng show how you can attract attention in a humorous and smart way and thus gain new customers. Their website is a portfolio of commissioned work, which was visualized in the style of an online fashion clothing store. Only at second glance do you see the main performers, the print products designed by the agency. The stylistic device here is a satirical and humorous look at the current visual trends in online presentation and online sales of fashion/clothing.

PRACTICE: *Take one of your (already completed) creative projects in hand and review the contents for any form of humor. Assuming it's not humorous, what would happen if you were to add a dash of irony to it? What happens to the contents? What does it mean? How is it changed? In your next project, you can decide to work satirically (that is, using irony, ridicule, and exaggeration to depict your views on a question or on a theme). What can you express satirically that cannot be communicated without this art form? What are the advantages and disadvantages of using satire?*

GET YOURSELF MOVING

Be it a walk around the block or a short exercise session, the main thing is movement! This is the motto for the next creative prescription. And It's also extremely simple: scientists at Stanford and Santa Clara Universities have found that you can greatly enhance your creative performance through physical movement. In their test, it made no difference whether the creative person was walking outdoors or moving at the same pace on a treadmill. Both had the same effect; if someone is in motion, there was a significantly higher output of creative performance. During the test, they also demonstrated that the (walking) movement has a continuing effect; that is, not only does more come to your mind while you are in motion, but you are also more creative after the walk than before.

Thus, being in motion (or after doing some physical exercise) can help you solve your creative tasks. Your creative output is greater, and your ideas might even be more innovative and unusual. When it comes to implementation (such as layout, production, the realization process, summoning up craftsmanship), movement is more of a hindrance if it's not part of the implementation itself. But it also applies here, that you should, if possible, take a break more often, get up, move around, spread out a bit and stretch, walk around, and then go back to work.

Before the start of a workshop or a teaching unit, I often try to get the participants activated by doing a short physical relaxation exercise. Especially if you are mentally active only afterwards, this can be very helpful for working and learning.

#
#StanfordUniversity
#SantaClaraUniversity
#Treadmill
#TakingAWalk
#GetYourselfMoving
#Activation

PRACTICE: *You are in the brainstorming phase. Instead of doing your brainstorming sitting down, walk around the room while you think. As you do this, write down your ideas on a handy notepad, dictate them into a recording device or call the ideas to a second person who will write them down for you while you keep moving.*

SURREALISM

The wonderful thing about creative ideas is that there are hardly any or no limits to the imagination. Anything you can imagine is possible, at least in principle! You can let animals speak, suddenly fly, walk on the ceiling, win the Nobel Prize, try out unusual culinary combinations, be immortal, invent impossible spaces and objects, declare the night to be day, have superpowers, create mythical creatures, bring the dead back to life, overcome space and time, and travel wherever you want. Great, isn't it?

Nºw you just have to decide what you feel like doing the most, because it could be difficult to do everything that is theoretically possible if you use your imagination and creativity. In combination, both imagination and creativity offer you infinite possibilities to let everything play itself out and to create surreal worlds.

Are you perhaps the second creative type *(see page 14)* who works virtuously and is a perfectionist, or the fourth creative type who approaches his or her tasks pragmatically and rationally? Then you will probably find it more difficult to create freely by drawing from within yourself and to imagine unreal or surreal scenarios. But that is exactly how I would ask you to work for this creative prescription! Simply give yourself the space to think up things that you would normally dismiss as "crazy." And the following applies to creative types 1 and 3: this is your playground. By using this method, you can simply do what you like doing anyway, which is let your imagination run wild and create things about which all non-creative people would say, "That just doesn't work. That's impossible!"

#Fantasy
#Flying
#Superpowers
#Surrealism
#SalvadorDalí
#M.C.Escher
#H.R.Giger
#JanVonHolleben

Salvador Dalí was one of the best-known representatives of the art genre of surrealism. He achieved fame above all for his paintings inspired by dreams and the unconscious. But later, various artists played with the subject of irrealism, such as the draftsman and graphic artist **M.C.Escher** with his impossible figures and spaces, or the artist **H.R.Giger**, who became famous mostly for his gloomy mechanoid representations (living beings that are half organic, half machine).

Jan von Holleben creates surreal image worlds by using his camera. At the same time, he works a bit like an illustrator does. The photographer describes himself as a kind of "Gyro Gearloose," an inventor of images, always on the lookout for new ideas for visualization. What is also striking is that he mostly seems to play with the viewer's perception. Reality is often shifted a bit, people and things are actors in unreal scenes, often staged in a poetic, humorous, tongue in cheek and intelligent way. His joy in trying something, experimenting, and spinning the picture around, is carried over to the viewer.

PRACTICE: *Dreamlike, unconscious, absurd, and fantastic: these are all features of surrealism. Can you incorporate one or more of these features into your creative work? Create a free (dream) project to let the surreal, irreal, fantastic, and what is far from realistic and any practicability run wild!*

PRESCRIPTION. №39

FIND ANALOGIES

With the help of analogies *(Greek analogía =* similarities, correspondence between two things; if two things are similar by means of one feature), you can look at your project and your creative idea from a different perspective.

An analogy can also be, in the figurative sense, something like a translation of your idea into another medium. For example, you have developed and sewn a handbag with a special clasp. Then you notice that this parti-cular clasp would also work for fastening a skirt or something else.

Or you look at something, and on the basis of that, come up with an idea for something completely different. You are developing an analogy, a completely new, revolutionary idea. This is what happens for many creative people. It's believed that the British graphic designer **Harry Beck**, who was employed as a draftsman in the signal department of the London **Underground**, looked at an electrical circuit diagram and used that to develop his iconic London Tube network map. This map was not concerned about being topographically accurate. Be-sides, Beck also represented each Tube line in its own color, and each line could only run in a horizontal or vertical direction, or along a 45° diagonal. This made it possible to cre-ate a very clear presentation, which has been copied many times over to this day.

Many analogies can be derived from nature. The field of bionics transfers natural phenomena into technical innovations; for example, the invention of the Velcro faste-ner, which came out of observing the cock-lebur plant; or the lotus effect, in which water beads up and rolls off surfaces.

#Similarities
#Translation
#HarryBeck
#Bionics
#VelcroFastener
#LotusEffect
#MuseumVisit
#YvonneKardel
#Dawanda
#KatharinaPreußer
#Youtube

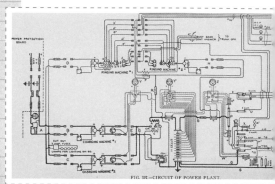

FIG. 207.—CIRCUIT OF POWER PLANT.

 **PRACTICE:** *Do you find analogies between your own creative output and that of someone you admire (see pages 98–98)? If so, how does that affect your own creative goals?*

DIY enthusiast **Yvonne Kardel** likes to sew unusual objects. One example of her handicraft skills is pin cushions in the shape of cacti, which she sells on the DaWanda creative platform! It's actually a very obvious analogy that Yvonne came across here! Cacti have spines (needles); a tailor sticks sewing needles in her or his pincushion for safe-keeping. The two together yield a pin cushion in the shape of a cactus!

Vlogger **Katharina Preußer** deals with returning to nature on her **YouTube** channel. In one video, she shows how she created her home-made birch shelves. Made of four slender birch tree trunks and some wooden boards and built in a jaunty way, including a few angles, she just might have incorporated the analogy of a "forest of books." The use of untreated wood can be seen as an analogy to the theme of "furniture made of wood or natural materials."

THINKING OUTSIDE THE BOX

Do you know the saying "Think outside the box"? I really like this phrase, because between the lines, it also describes how you should be open to new things and should not just revolve around yourself. Rather, it encourages you to step out of your own focus, without leaving it behind entirely. And without a specific goal in mind, you look at what others are working on and how they work to derive something for your creative way of working.

"Thinking outside the box" also means transferring functioning systems from other fields into your own field and adapting them. An example of how this can work is making use of idle self-service devices in publicly accessible places. It's possible to build twenty-four-hour art vending machines—that is, individual art dispensing machines—from old, purely mechanical and outdated cigarette- dispensing machines. And vacant, enclosed telephone booths are being used more and more to set up "micro-libraries," where people can bring the books they have finished reading or take out books and then bring them back again if necessary.

\#

\#OutsideTheBox
\#BeyondYourOwnField
\#Interdisciplinary
\#ArtVendingMachine
\#Micro-Library
\#PublicBookshelf
\#Tat-O-Mat
\#Tatendrang-Design
\#Upcycling

Example of a microlibrary or a public bookshelf in an old telephone booth in Braunschweig, Germany.

While I was studying, I bought an old cigarette machine together with some fellow students and turned it into an art vending machine. For several years now, I have been running five art-vending machines in Braunschweig with **Tatendrang-Design®**.

The regional art scene, which is able to participate in this networking project, benefits from it, just like the customers of vending-machine art, the citizenry and tourists who enjoy buying a work of art and a souvenir from the changing assortment in the machines for a small amount of money.

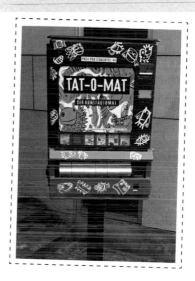

PRACTICE: _Look at an exhibition in a museum of your choice. Can you derive, transfer, or adapt something for your work from the exhibited objects? How would the new influences affect your own creative output?_

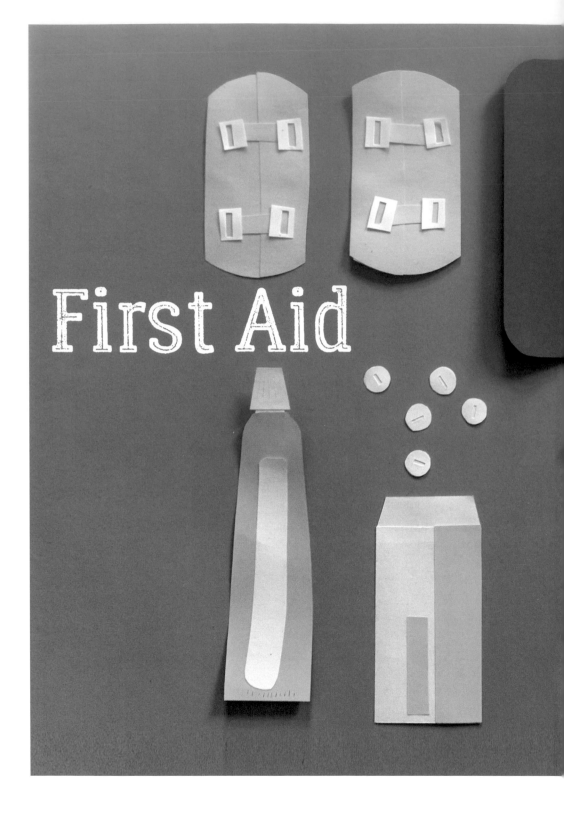

First Aid

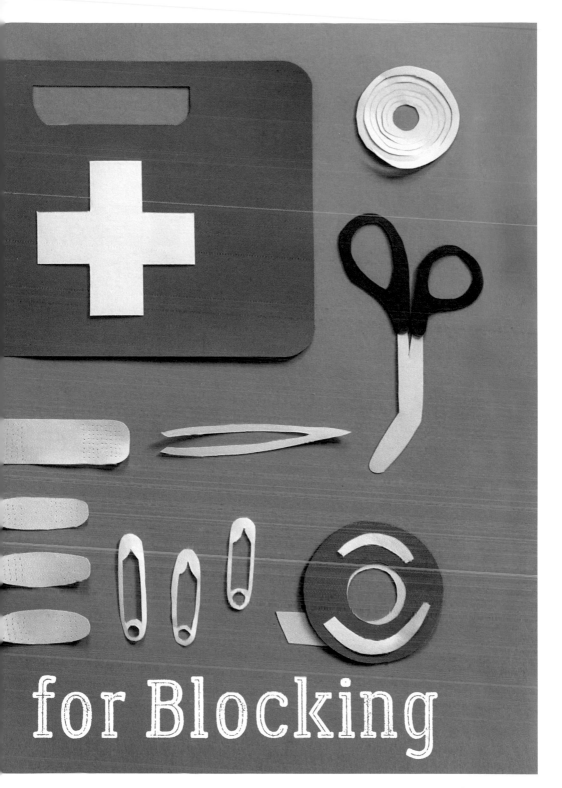

for Blocking

Recognizing & Analyzing Blocking

If things aren't going so well for your creative power, then you are probably blocked. All creative people suffer from this now and then. There are often manifold reasons for it. Before you can research the causes, you first have to become aware of the problem and recognize the blocking as such! That might sound trivial, but some creative people ignore the first signs, force themselves to keep on working, and become stressed and overwhelmed. That, in turn, can make you sick.

> **"You don't have stress, you make it yourself."**
>
> Aba Assa

It's therefore important to listen to the signals, to be aware of your own blocking, and then to accept it (otherwise the situation will become stressful) and ultimately to try to overcome it. In order to resolve the problem completely and to prevent further blocking, you should first analyze where the block came from. Stress on a private/professional level can be one reason why you can no longer live a free and serene creative life. Persistent, negative stress leads to excessive demands (yes, there is also positive stress, and this can be very beneficial to your creativity). Other stress factors can include managing time too narrowly, unrealistic goals, exaggerated ambition and a too-small budget or a potential financial squeeze.

Any conscious or unconscious unwellness of body or mind can trigger blocking. This can have purely physical causes (such as sickness), or it can be triggered by external factors such as being disturbed by noise, the wrong lighting, a sub-optimal workplace, or adverse cooperation with others.

Even unconscious feelings of guilt (such as worries or moral concerns) can cause you to block. At the same time, 90% of the things we worry about don't come to pass! Worrying about things shows a pronounced fantasy and sometimes even an indecision to tackle things. If you were to postpone things less, you might have to worry less.

Fear can also be reason for blocking. Sadness, rage, and anger are also considered to be destructive, since these are negative emotions that absorb a lot of your energy and make relaxed and creative work almost impossible. Instead, they paralyze you and prevent a free spirit, which is a basic requirement for creative people.

Recognize and Analyze Your Situation

Step 1: Recognize that "something is not going well."
To do this, you need to be mindful.

Step 2: Analyze where the blocking is coming from.
Things that trigger a creative block could be:
- Stress (physical & mental);
- Not feeling well;
- Worry & anxiety;
- Sadness, rage, anger;
- Perfectionism & over-motivation;
- Criticism (self-criticism and criticism from others);
- Self-doubt & insecurity & feelings of inferiority;
- Lack of time and money.

Perfectionism and a lack of critical capability, destructive criticism, or too harsh self-criticism are also significant triggers for blocking.

I would like to add one more thing: every creative person becomes blocked or makes mistakes or encounters obstacles or headwinds at one time or another. This is completely normal and is (unfortunately) part of creative activity. Yet we can also get the better of this!

On the following pages you will find 15 first aid tips for various blocking situations and creativity killers. These tips can help you to quickly overcome blocking and get back into the creative flow.

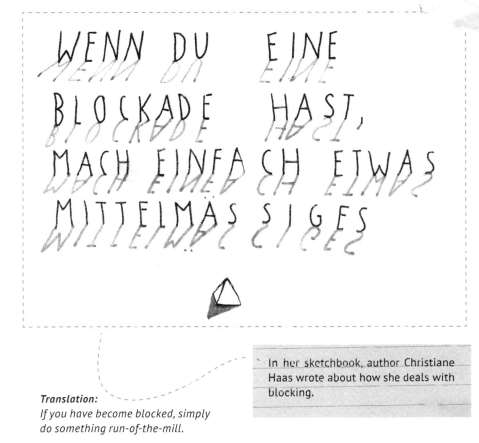

WENN DU EINE
BLOCKADE HAST,
MACH EINFACH ETWAS
MITTELMÄSSIGES

In her sketchbook, author Christiane Haas wrote about how she deals with blocking.

Translation:
If you have become blocked, simply do something run-of-the-mill.

Be Brave, Jump In

Diagnosis:

Fear, doubt, uncertainty, fear of a blank page.

Medical History:

Blocking is often caused by fear. The fear of embarrassing your-self, of being and remaining uni-maginative, of not satisfying yourself and others, of your work being bad, of failing—these are the most common fears related to a creative block.

First of all, being afraid is a natural reaction of the body, a protective mechanism. So don't panic! First and foremost, fear alerts you to a problem or tricky situation. You can work with this kind of mindfulness. But fear is always destructive, while positive stress can still have a constructive effect. If it has such a grip on you that the fear constrains, paralyzes, or prevents you from being active, then you should get to the bottom of what is causing it. If the fear is unfounded, then you should face this and fight it rationally, to get yourself out of the constraints or blocking.

In many cases, the thought of chan-ging your current situation and the beha-vior associated with it is perceived as behavior that you should change and that is intolerable for you. The reason for this

> ## Fears that may occur in creative people:
> - the fear that nothing will come to mind (blackout);
> - the fear of making a mistake;
> - the fear of uncertainty;
> - the fear of stress and excessive demands;
> - the fear of your own inability;
> - the fear of your own failure;
> - the fear of exposing yourself;
> - the fear of criticism;
> - the fear of rejection, or even a social comedown;
> - the fear of consequences (legal, financial).

is the fear of uncertainty and the lack of courage to change. Most people must first feel the pressure of suffering before they change their behavior. For this reason, it can happen that you first remain blocked, like a deer blinded by headlights in the road, instead of taking countermeasures.

Some creative people also block themselves or give up too easily, not because they could not perform or accom-plish the work but because they are afraid of being appraised or judged. They are afraid of criticism and rejection.

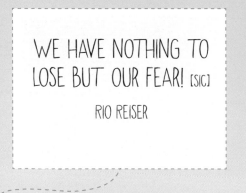

WE HAVE NOTHING TO
LOSE BUT OUR FEAR! [SIC]

RIO REISER

Type of First Aid and Prescribed Treatment:

+ Have a positive attitude. Be brave and just do it! If you think about things too much, you may also build up more fears and worry unnecessarily. Taking the first step in a project is the step that requires the most courage. But if you succeed in that, then you have won half the battle! Have some confidence in yourself and say to yourself something like: "What others can do, I can too!"

+ Come to terms with your fear. Face your fear, take it on and fight against it. Fear can help take your creativity to the next level and propel you to better performance by defeating it. Don't see it as an invincible opponent.

+ Formulate your next steps in writing in a few sentences. Avoid formulations such as, "I'll try this and that." Replace this with a specific choice of words, such as "I will do this and that." The way we formulate something determines whether we are successful in dealing with it.

+ Give a name to the obstacles that are standing in your way (and blocking you). When you express them in words, you can find strategies to overcome them more easily!

+ Lose your fear of the blank piece of paper by starting with a finger exercise from your creative area to warm up. It's important that something visible is created. Congratulations, you have gotten started! Now you can slowly change over to the actual primary task.

+ Don't forget to have fun! Release tension by envisioning the fun you are having. Or look at things with the naivety of a child, being less critical.

+ Call it an experiment (not a project), because this will take some of the pressure off the expectations when you talk to others about it.

Get Out of Your Comfort Zone

№2

Diagnosis:

Lack of imagination, too much routine, complacency, laziness.

Medical History:

As a rule, blocking can always be treated by making a change in your everyday life/daily business. Broadening your horizons, gaining new experiences, and building up a wealth of knowledge will help you become open to creative influences, because a change in everyday life makes it possible to generate new ideas!

You can have new experiences by doing things such as leaving your familiar surroundings and thus your comfort zone. By comfort zone, I mean not just the place where you do your creative work, but also your inner attitude towards it. You probably have a certain routine in approaching projects (and that's good and important, too). But sometimes, it can make sense, especially if you're only getting average results or are not satisfied with your performance, to consciously break this routine and try out things that are very difficult for you at first. Trust yourself! Try it! Give yourself the opportunity to enhance your mental flexibility and to take a new pathway. Brief trips, new events, travel, a vacation, spontaneous events, or a small adventure can give you new impressions and perspectives for your creative work. Or take the time to learn new things, to further educate yourself (workshops, courses, lectures, specialist books, online tutorials, webinars, etc.). Expand your awareness and thus your future creative possibilities. If you exchange the familiar for the unknown, you will have new experiences. In this way you can break out of your striving for control, stability, and security, which constrains your creativity and is given to everyone by nature as a protective mechanism. Another tip: ideas often come to you exactly where you least expect them!

Type of First Aid and Prescribed Treatment:

+ *Get involved in something completely new!* This can be anything possible: a trip, a workshop, a theme that you have avoided so far, a place where you've never been, a secret wish that you are now bringing into being. Be spontaneous and curious. Let yourself be carried away and surprised by the situation.

Jan Augsberg quit his supposedly secure job as an architect in 2016 in order to embark on a journey into the unknown. With the rough goal in mind of playing 100 concerts in 100 different cities, he set out. He had barely any concert experience, no contacts in the music business, and beyond that, he didn't know how to organize a concert tour. On December 23, 2016, he gave his 100th concert in Berlin, with 70,000 km, two continents, and sixteen countries lying in his wake. Why did he venture on this journey despite all the uncertainties? He says: "I think I wanted to find out more about myself, about life, about people."

Type of First Aid and Prescribed Treatment:

+ Put something at risk! The pursuit of security inhibits your creative potential. You cannot draw on unlimited resources with the emergency brake on. Trust yourself and leave your comfort zone (*see also Prescription № 40, page 110*). It will be worth the (small) risk.

+ Change your inner mindset/attitude. Being biased and having prejudices can keep you away from enriching experiences. Be open and unbiased! You should likewise fight complacency and laziness!

+ Don't take the pathway you always take! You can take this literally as well as understand it figuratively. The way is sometimes the goal.

+ If you can't make it, fake it! And fake it until you make it! Starting a new creative chapter is not easy for anyone. That's why you can calmly use a little trickery and "pretend to do things"; the main thing is that you don't let yourself be dissuaded so quickly. Because then the "pretending" becomes "I'll do it and I can!"

+ Express your ideas ("unlaid eggs")! That will help you actually implement them, along the lines of: "Now that I've said it, now I have to do it, too!" Make an idea even more binding by writing it down like an appointment in your calendar.

+ Change your location! If you are blocking, find another place to work (perhaps a place that is unusual, contrary, or unknown for you).

The Right Timing

## 3

Diagnosis:

Time pressure, excessive demands, stress.

Medical History:

If you are stressed because of time pressure or you are overwhelmed by a big task, try to plan your time a bit. Don't be afraid of being constrained or "clocked in" by planning your time; the opposite is the case. With good scheduling, you gain time and thus freedom, because planning your time means being more effective in less time and thus working in a smarter way instead of working harder. You set your goals and your priorities, and then you "only" have to carry them out.

If you are overwhelmed by a project, it may be because its scope is too great or you haven't planned enough time for it. This in turn can stress you and possibly make you block. One way to make large projects clearer is to use the milestone method. To do this, you divide up and break down your complex project into smaller steps. That is, you split it into parts and define milestones (intermediate goals) that you clearly name as part of the project and want to achieve in a certain phase of the project. In your milestone schedule, you define all the interim goals as milestones and, in the best case, build in buffer zones (so that you can sometimes go overboard and are prepared for incidents, the unforeseen, and surprises). The advantage of this is that you don't have to constantly be thinking about the whole project; instead, you just have to concentrate on the next step. This way, you get to your goal bit by bit.

It's important to know that the first and the last milestones are the most difficult! Once you've gotten started, the next steps will be easier for you. In my experience, the last milestone requires the most energy from you, and usually this is more than you originally planned on. Here you should plan in a lot of buffer time to ensure you complete it successfully.

There are other things to consider when planning your time: When do you work best (time of day, span of time during the day)? Observe your creative curve and adjust your daily planning accordingly—this way you work more efficiently. Can you set priorities? Which actions and tasks in the daily creative process or in your work are urgent; which are important? Can you say no? And are you able to realistically assess when tasks will become too much for you, which projects, competitions, collaborations, inquiries, and so on will help you advance and benefit you, and which you are better off rejecting, because the effort and the benefit are not in proportion?

Type of First Aid and Prescribed Treatment:

+   *Keep a diary and figure out what time you waste.* Keep a diary for a week and write down how long you spend your time on various things. You will be surprised that there are some time wasters that take up more time than you had previously realized. You can avoid them during the next step, so that you will have time for important and beautiful things! Also interesting: Where have you wasted other people's time and where have others wasted your time? Can you change that?

+   *Include time for yourself (such as time to relax or for things that are important to you).* As part of your timing diary, you can also analyze when you had time just for yourself. Is this enough time for you? Can you set a daily or weekly appointment for it (for example, every Monday 9–10 a.m., fifteen minutes a day, or something similar). It's important to have time to reflect and relax.

+   *Establish a list of daily tasks.* The day before, write down a list of what (such as phone calls, work on projects, sports, shopping) you would like to do and when for the next day. Then you won't have to think about it tomorrow. The list will also help you avoid distracting yourself with unimportant activities. You don't need to adhere to this list slavishly; figure out how much time meets your needs. It's perfectly fine if sometimes things don't go "according to plan" or if you haven't dealt with all the items on that day.

+   *A backward error analysis* can solve mental blocks. Forget your blocks for a moment and sketch out your desired project results, such as its successful conclusion. Mentally work your way backwards (possibly also together with a discussion partner) from this goal, going step by step through the various phases of work, until you have arrived back at your current problem. Perhaps this process has given you a new perspective for resolving the block.

+   *Use waiting times.* Regardless of whether you are sitting in the doctor's waiting room or on the train, this is time that you can use for active relaxation or for being creative. You can write, listen to music, read, or think over a problem. In any case, be sure to pack something to write with.

+   *Value the present!* Do not regret the past and do not be afraid of the future; you cannot influence either and it only costs you energy.

There's No Such Thing as Perfection!

## 4

Diagnosis:

Perfectionism, over-motivation, failures.

Medical History:

It's a generally widespread view in society that perfection is something worth striving for. We're brought up to do our best, so that we can be the best in a field. At the same time, this is totally unrealistic, almost unattainable, and therefore frustrating. And this striving does not necessarily promote innovation because it first and foremost involves status rather than a goal with substance.

You should preferably strive for making outstanding achievements and self-actualization in areas that you enjoy doing and that mean something to you.

If you want to be the best, this means that you are constantly comparing yourself to others, and I would bet you only compare yourself to those whom you consider to be "better" than you are, right? Thus, your self-certified failure becomes quite likely. German author **Petra Bock** calls this a classic "mindfuck," which eventually blocks you mentally. It's typical human behavior to overestimate others and devalue yourself in the process. But viewed rationally, no person is perfect. Rather, you should accept yourself for who you are, with all your strengths and weaknesses. Everyone makes mistakes. What is important is to recognize them so that you can correct them and not make them a second time.

You can learn from mistakes and thus improve, step by step.

Mistakes, failures, and having things flop are part of things, but aren't a prerequisite. Don't get discouraged if you make mistakes. Instead, tell yourself: a previous failure can definitely contribute significantly to success in the future. If you want to be more successful, you have to be prepared to fail more often, if necessary.

So that you don't become blocked in the first place, don't judge how well you are doing something right when you are doing it; just do it. That is the first and most important thing! You will have enough time later to take a critical look at it, to improve it, to change it, or to discard it entirely. It has been demonstrated that in the early stages of the creative process, it's better to come up with many concepts than to generate *the one* perfect idea. In this phase, quantity is more important than quality. And one trick to curb your own demand for perfection is not taking things as being so important from the beginning and to approach the task casually. For reassurance, you can also tell yourself that mediocrity is nothing to be ashamed about; it's normal. There are very few people who are the total high-flyers and absolutely brilliant—they are the exception, and there are very, very few such people!

FAILURE FUCKS. BUT INSTRUCTS.

PROF. BOB SUTTON & DIEGO RODRIGUEZ

Personal resilience, courage and humility, that grow out of beneficial defeats, are of inestimable value for maturing and personality development.

Chris Flink

Type of First Aid and Prescribed Treatment:

+ Do everything with your left hand! If you use the "wrong" hand to do everything (brushing your teeth, buttering bread, writing, telephoning, etc.) for one day, you will find that you have to perform every move in a more conscious way. You have a different focus, and you get to know the things you are doing anew. This perspective can help you, so that you don't take your everyday life and your skills for granted. Besides, you are stimulating the other half of your brain and thus your creative thinking—at the same time, you are encouraged to be less of a perfectionist.

+ Create a list of things you do competently. To increase your self-esteem, you can make a list of your competences: What do you do well? What are your special skills and what do you do competently? Emphasize your "pros." At this point, neglect your weaknesses and the "cons." Celebrate your strengths!

+ Fuck-up event. Attend or host a "fuck-up" event, a meeting/event about failures where people gather to share how they have failed and what mistakes they made. You can learn from their experiences and use this environment to review your own expectations.

+ Take children as role models because they don't think about perfection when they play. They simply just do things.

Find Rituals

## 5

Diagnosis:

Being distracted, lack of concentration, struggling with your "inner Schweinehund."

Medical History:

Every creative person is ready to do (almost) anything to get into the creative flow and to stay there for as long as possible. Woody Allen, for example, realized that it gives him a new boost every time he changes his room in his apartment. As soon as he notices that his creative flow (for writing scripts) is becoming more limited, he changes rooms (again). And, he says, taking a shower in the middle of the day helps. After all, the bathroom is a different room, and he is able to think well in the shower.

Over time, the experience in dealing with your own creativity will show you individual behavior patterns, habits, and rituals that will help you get yourself into the creative flow, quickly and professionally. You will also develop preferences that you (sometimes supposedly) need to be creative in the best way and to establish a relative sense of well-being (work rituals, location, music, talismans, and so on). When I am writing, for example, I always sit at a table, and things have to be very calm and quiet around me (music doesn't work at all!) If, on the other hand, I am drawing or painting, I can do it anywhere, as long as

there is music! A friend of mine is a journalist, who writes all of his texts sitting up in his bed with his laptop on his lap.

Once you have become used to your habits and rituals, you can sometimes become blocked if you fail to do them, if you are not at your usual workplace, or if the day goes differently than usual. Then observe your behavior: Exactly why are you blocking right now? What could help you habitually so that you no longer become blocked? Can you try to get into a flow mood even without these rituals or your familiar surroundings? And what do you need for that?

Everyone is different. Some people need variety and find rituals, habits, and routines to be stifling. But at this point, just look at yourself, at what you like and what helps you, since there is no general prescription for all.

If you are blocking, it can help you to create a ritual to break down the block again. Unfortunately, you have to find out for yourself what that is (such as get out of the situation, talk to someone, physical exercise, go for a walk, eat, sleep, drink, meditate, or go to the movies).

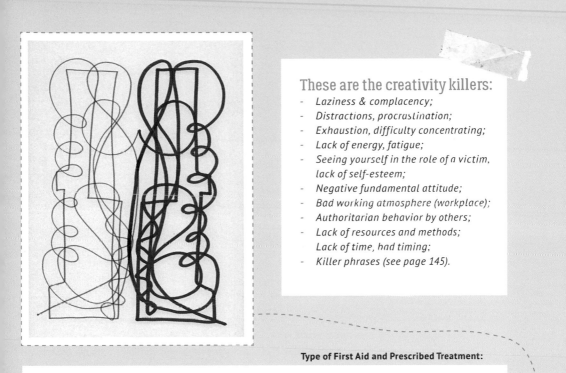

Type of First Aid and Prescribed Treatment:

+ *Avoid interruptions.* To remain in the flow and to keep your concentration, it's important that you don't interrupt yourself or that others don't interrupt your creative activity. Make sure in advance that there will be no interference.

+ *Prevent avoidance actions.* When you shy away from a new task and let yourself become blocked, you may (like many people) tend to perform displacement activities, such as cleaning or tidying up your desk in a hectic way, all just to avoid the task. This is not a ritual (but it can become a habit). If you notice this behavior, suppress it and force yourself to tackle the new task. You can trick yourself, in fact, and act according to the reward principle: "When I have accomplished this task, I may do . . . as a reward."

+ *Synchronized drawing to loosen up.* If you are blocking, take a sheet of 11x16 paper and two pens of your choice. Fasten the sheet of paper to the surface so that it cannot slip away. Then draw a symmetrical figure with both hands in the form of fluid movements, such as a line. Do not consciously pay attention to what you are doing. This exercise activates both sides of the brain and makes you more relaxed for the creative work that follows. For advanced people: do the same exercise but have each hand drawing something different at the same time!

Turn Negative into Positive

## 6

Diagnosis:

Rage, anger, frustration (strong feelings).

Medical History:

Blocking comes from within ourselves. It does not arise from others. Your subconscious is the key and the driving force. It decides whether you take a relaxed approach to a task, achieve a goal with ease or make it difficult for yourself, block yourself and sabotage things. In principle, you are your own friend and your own enemy at the same time. Your inner attitude determines how you deal with problems/tasks. How can you communicate with your subconscious and influence it? (I hope I can offer a variety of suggested solutions for this in this "First Aid" chapter!) One tip is certainly to have a positive inner attitude regarding a problem or a task and in regard to your own creative abilities. Creative success depends heavily upon inner peace, confidence, and a positive mindset. But how do you specifically deal with negative situations (such as your own outrage over injustices, destructive criticism, stupidity, lack of understanding, killer phrases)? The first impulse is to have strong negative feelings anger and frustration) that can block you and make you unsure of yourself. One way to regain your objectivity and relaxation is to work against them in a positive and constructive way. For example, say to yourself: "I can still get upset about that tomorrow."

Or you first count to ten and take a deep breath and slowly exhale as you count. If that doesn't help, you can say to yourself: "Now more than ever!" The negative energy can be used and converted into a positive energy boost for your project. Because rage and anger have creative potential. Your self-confidence can undo any toxic effects of a lousy killer phrase! If you can't do it of your own accord, then you can "use it" with someone else; someone you want to prove this to, or who would be helped by it. If this doesn't work either, then first remove yourself from the situation and let the anger and rage out elsewhere, such as by sports or other purely physical activities. You can express yourself instead in another creative medium and use this as a safety valve (if you are a designer, for example through music or writing; never stay in the same medium).

Perhaps it will comfort you a bit that, in my experience (and certainly also in the experience of many others), situations that annoy you, frustrate you and pull you down can often act more as creative catalysts than positive situations would be able to do so.

Type of First Aid and Prescribed Treatment:

+   That would be something to laugh at! Humor is a means of dealing elegantly and aggressively with criticism and killer phrases. This way, you don't take criticism too seriously, especially if it's obviously only intended to devalue you or to nip your idea in the bud.

And you should be able to laugh at yourself, too! Humor helps create distance from situations where you may have lost your way. If you have a sense of humor, you are showing that you have brains and stature at the same time.

+   Make a virtue out of necessity. When you are trapped in a negative mood, you find yourself in emotional distress. Necessity is the mother of invention! Make the best of your situation, make use of the conditions that are currently available to you, and this may even result in a shortcut to your goal that you had not even seen before!

+   How about a motivational mantra? If you are having doubts about yourself or your abilities (or are very angry right now), say to yourself out loud: "Who, if not me? When, if not now? Where, if not here? What, if not this exactly? How, if not exactly this way?"

+   Are you frustrated because you are not doing everything that you actually want to do and that really fulfills you? Compile a "bucket list" and write down everything you still would like to experience and achieve, no matter how silly or unrealistic. Afterwards, try to work through it gradually. And remember, success is a skill that you can learn; you are certainly at your most successful when you do what you love and what you really want to do.

Willpower, Perseverance & Continuity

№7

Diagnosis:

Demotivation, lack of fighting spirit.

Medical History:

If you lack willpower, then feelings of displeasure, distractions, and other obstacles often get in the way and block you from reaching your goals. So, what do you do when there is too little "strength of will"? You have to learn to focus on your goal, to be able to set priorities, to be willing to take risks, and not to let obstacles and the unforeseen dissuade you from your goal. You should furthermore be able to plan ahead. It's also important to tackle and solve problems before they become too big and ultimately jeopardize the achievement of your goal. Incidentally, the latter is called the Niagara Syndrome. Think of it this way; you are paddling along a river until the current (Niagara Falls) becomes a serious problem that you can no longer deal with your muscular strength (compare to your willpower). Besides this, you should also learn to trust yourself more (self-confidence!) and to act in a goal-oriented, independently, and self-disciplined way.

Many creative people have additional competence in the area of willpower. They can influence their own feelings and moods in such a way that they can muster up more mental energy than they actually need, which means that their store of energy (willpower) is always so full that there is no danger of giving up their goal. They program themselves with positive thoughts and firmly believe that they can do what has to be done.

Your willpower is defined by character traits such as perseverance (tenacity), robustness, drive, determination, and single-mindedness. If you have these "superpowers," you can achieve the goals you have set for yourself without having to fight against too much resistance.

Type of First Aid and Prescribed Treatment:

+ *Train yourself in a new behavior.* They say it takes twenty-one days to train yourself in a new behavior before it becomes customary and finally becomes "flesh and blood." It's essential that you stick to it consistently and willingly, not allowing any exceptions, and above all, no excuses.

Type of First Aid and Prescribed Treatment:

I think everyone knows this from sports: you plan to exercise more, sign up for a fitness studio, and go there regularly for the first three to four weeks. You are proud and happy. But then it subsides, and your baser instinct wins, once, twice; then you go again and then you don't. You don't get into a routine, and the goal becomes nothing. You have let things slide and feel like a loser who lost the battle with herself or himself. There's only one thing to do (and that's hard, because nobody likes to hear it): it's all in your own hands. If you really want to, you can also achieve it. You can do anything you really, really want to do.

+ *Practice makes perfect here, too.* As already written in *Prescription Nº. 24*, nothing works without practice. But where there's a will, there's a way, and constant practice brings improvement. Creative abilities are like muscles that develop through exercise and become stronger through endurance; continuous training (steadiness) then keeps them in shape (here we are back to sports again). And once again, take note: working creatively, creatively drawing from within yourself, is work (regardless of whether as an artist, musician, cook, freelancer, entrepreneur, writer, do-it-yourselfer, or whatever)!

+ *Always keep getting up again.* When you've experienced defeat, it's important not to let it destroy you mentally. As a friend of mine says in such moments: "Fall down, get up, put your hat on straight, move on." You can compensate for unsuccessful attempts and defeats with perseverance and determination. And at some point, it will definitely work.

+ *A free ride, please!* To be able to work well creatively, you must not let yourself be restricted in your scope or your freedom. Give yourself a mental free ride for what you are doing, so that you are able to try things out. Take all the freedom you need and don't let yourself be guided by external expectations and don't censor yourself.

Support

№8

Diagnosis:

Reaching your own limits, standstill.

Medical History:

You may possibly get to a point in your creative work where you won't be able to get any further if you don't get help. Stress factors can overwhelm you because you are not an expert at dealing with them. The tip here is to outsource these immediately and hand them over to a helpful expert. This is how you successfully minimize your stressors. The advantages of working with a supporter are obvious. Four eyes see more than two; four hands can get more done than two. If you work as a pair, you will expand and complement each other's creative abilities and skills. If the temporary support becomes a partnership—or if it's one from the start *(see page 64)*—you are also sharing the risk and the financial investment. This makes things easier for both partners and represents a clear advantage over being a "lone fighter." Besides, teamwork will also elicit social responsibility among yourselves and further advance your project, along the lines of: "I definitely don't want to leave my partner in the lurch."

With temporary support, you can turn the problem that triggered the blocking into a problem for someone else for a while.

You share the burden, and your helper or yourself may find a new way to solve the problem. An outsider who offers you help looks at the problem with a different perspective than you (the insider) do. That can be crucial.

A supporter can also be a sparring partner for you *(see page 72)*. It's important that he or she knows your situation exactly and can empathize with you. One potential way of sparring could be as follows: Explain the problem to them. They should put what has been said in writing. From this, they then develop questions. From these, you derive answers together that represent possible solutions to the problem.

Mental support should likewise not be underestimated. This does not involve any specific, present supporter; rather, this involves your mental well-being. Surround yourself with people who understand, support, motivate, show empathy, and if necessary, are themselves dealing with something similar. On the other hand, indifferent, negative-thinking and argumentative people are taboo for you.

+ ***A conscious decision to seek help!*** Already, the decision to seek help and support can solve the block or at least elicit a small change in your way of thinking.

+ ***Obtain a professional opinion.*** Ask experts about their opinion regarding your work/problem, etc., especially people you don't know! There are many opportunities to do this, such as a portfolio review, a go-see, a casting, a writing or cooking seminar, or a conference. The opinions of outside experts are particularly interesting and helpful for you because they do not know you and may be able to judge objectively and impartially.

+ ***Motivator.*** Consciously seek something that motivates or encourages you, such as at a (workshop) discussion with like-minded people, at specialist lectures, forums, in Facebook groups, or from a specialist book. It has never been easier than it is today to make direct worldwide contacts via the internet. In exchanges you can tell each other about projects, successes, obstacles, and resistance; seek advice; and encourage each other.

+ ***Just ask.*** Many people shy away from asking for help, and it seems even more difficult to speak to someone you don't know. My advice here too: make things simple! Whether it's in person, by telephone, or by email, introduce yourself briefly, communicate clearly and in a friendly manner what you need/want to know, and then wait. I am always surprised by the very normal way such an exchange works (regardless of whether it's with a luminary, train attendant, tax office employee, member of an organization, or whatever).

+ ***A network gives you security and creates relationships.*** Build up a network (or find an existing network) that understands you and your creative ideas, takes you further, and maybe even provides you with support. The larger the network is, the greater the chance of finding help and support within it and of building useful relationships. Also, don't underestimate word of mouth. The world is small. Perhaps someone knows someone, who knows someone, who can help you!

+ ***Get active.*** Approach people and don't wait to be discovered or for someone to come up to you and offer you help.

Set Boundaries

Diagnosis:

You've lost the thread/overview, are getting bogged down,
limited budget/not enough time

Medical History:

Taking on tasks and projects whose degree of difficulty is too high and that have a scope and duration difficult to gauge are typical problems for many creative people. And that's not necessarily a mistake only beginners make. Of course, over time you learn to better assess and appreciate tasks, but nevertheless, it's sometimes only over the course of the project that some activities turn out to be guzzlers of time, budget, and competence, even for people who do advanced creative work. If the creative project is too complex, it might happen that you become desperate, lose your overview, get bogged down, and, at some point, become totally frustrated and blocked as a result. By now, you should step in and draw boundaries, or otherwise your work on the project will become ineffective and inefficient.

On one hand, you can use the "milestone method" (see page 120), but that doesn't really constrain you. It only gives greater oversight and structure to your creative project, which reduces the risk of getting bogged down. By "constraining," I mean that you permanently subtract something from your task. Can you reduce the budget (this may reduce your risk, if any, and mean fewer items that you have to finance or that have to be funded)? Can you allot yourself less time to do the task?

What kind of consequences would that have? When you have less time, the project must be automatically simplified, shrunk/boiled down, so that you can still get it done. Is that perhaps better for the overall result, which is your goal? For the free time that will remain to you, that would definitely be true. Can you limit the project to the extent that you have to invest less manpower, and that it costs you and any potential other people involved (employees, temporary workers, et al.) less effort? Less manpower may mean more potential profit for the remaining participants—although "profit" does not necessarily have to have something to do with money. That is a clear advantage!

Too much freedom for doing a task can block you. Set boundaries (for yourself) if you are overwhelmed by your own demands. Through this process, you can become more creative! These could be thematic, material, format-related, or formal boundaries. Perhaps you narrow down your theme even further (make it more specific), decide on a few tools and materials and think of everything in a simpler way (for example, as an illustrator you only produce simple line drawings instead of elaborate, painterly pictures).

Less is more.
(Weniger ist mehr.)

The expression "less is more" became popular among architects, designers, and artists in the early twentieth century. **Ludwig Mies van der Rohe**, the architect and director of the Bauhaus school of design in Dessau, Germany, took up this formulation again (he did not invent it) to describe his conception of building construction. Van der Rohe preferred plain, simple shapes and rejected decorative ornamentation. He was thus one of the minimalists.

Type of First Aid and Prescribed Treatment:

+ *Work through constraints conceptually.* Sometimes it's already sufficient to imagine a limitation of your resources. Ask yourself: What would happen if you only had half the time? Then what would you concentrate on? What would happen if you only had half the budget? What could you do without?

+ *Constrain your senses!* Depending on what you are doing, you can constrain one (or more) of your senses in order to overcome a block or lack of focus. Your other, unconstrained senses will thus become sharper, your concentration will increase, and you will focus yourself better. Distractions will then have less of an impact.

For example, If you are writing and can't concentrate, put ear plugs in your ears. When you need to think things over but cannot think clearly, close your eyes and ears. Sometimes, it also makes sense to hold your nose or breathe through your mouth, as if something stinks or has an offensive smell and as a result you can no longer concentrate.

+ *Limit yourself to what is simplest.* Sometimes the problems seem so intertwined with each other that they seem unsolvable as a result. This leaves you in despair and blocked. Seek out the simplest part of a problem—it should be one that you can tackle right away—and resolve it. The first step is taken.

+ *"Constraining yourself" does not mean stopping something completely!* Of course, you have the option at any time to pull the ripcord and say "stop" if you think something is no longer worth striving for or is no longer feasible. Nº question! But don't give up too soon. The stage before surrender should be "constraining yourself." Perhaps you will save a great project by doing this!

Time Out for Body and Spirit

№10

Diagnosis:

Lack of energy, demotivation, emptiness

> ## SLEEPING IS THE HEIGHT OF GENIUS.
>
> ### KIERKEGAARD

Medical History:

After high-performance creative work, it's normal and human that your battery will run down at some point. The energy and the urge to create have gone on their way. You are tired, unconcentrated, and erratic. Perhaps you would like to go on working for a little while, but you just can't do anything anymore. Both your body and your mind need to relax to recharge your batteries.

Take a break! Because when you relax physically, this is carried over to your state of mind as well. Your behavior influences your state of consciousness, and you gather new strength and impulses for further creative work. A positive mood and relaxation lead to enhanced creativity in everyone. Physical relaxation is anything that is good for you personally, your body needs and increases your well-being: eating, drinking, reading, sleeping, bathing, taking a shower, daydreaming, exercise, love, sex, going for a walk, cycling, looking for some diversion, meeting friends, looking at something (nature, art, culture), and so forth.

Another way to relax body and mind through your downtime is to use a range of relaxation techniques: progressive muscle relaxation, deep relaxation, meditation, or autogenic training. You can also try "turning your head off" and doing absolutely nothing—although this is a very difficult exercise, at least if you remain conscious. If you don't remain conscious, however, then you are sleeping (one hopes). But even in your sleep, you are rarely doing nothing. In your dreams you work through your everyday life and become quite creative in the process. In the dream you will become a true improvisational artist. Do you know the saying, "Sleep on it?" It means that, with the help of sleep, you let a decision sink in one more time, and gain emotional distance. The next day you scrutinize your decision one last time with a fresh, relaxed mind before you make a binding decision.

A daydream is the awakened and more conscious version of a night dream. This, too, can help you clarify something and to relax at the same time.

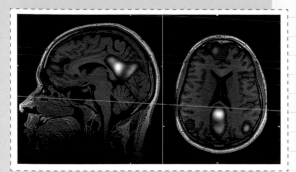

In 2001, neuroscientists discovered the *"default-mode network" (DMN)* in the human brain. This term describes a group of brain regions that become active when you are doing nothing and are inactive or deactivated when solving tasks. The DMN becomes more active when a person is daydreaming, forging plans for the future, and so forth. It also enables us to do so-called "stimulus-independent thinking."

Type of First Aid and Prescribed Treatment:

+ *Prescribe yourself a break (more often)!* While doing creative work, you tend to exploit yourself because you "creatively draw from within yourself." And because you are with yourself twenty-four hours a day, there is always at least the risk of "continuing to create," although you could have used some regenerating downtime long ago. Submissions/deadlines can only reinforce this effect. It's therefore important that you realize in good time that it's time to take a break before you become completely exhausted. At best, downtime should alternate with creative time in such a way that they balance each other out or that you become balanced as a result. Another positive effect for you: this isn't an actual break from creativity. During your break, you unconsciously continue to brood over your creative idea. So take the time you need!

+ *Accept and enjoy your downtime!* Perhaps you, like many others, tend not to allow yourself this break. And your conscience is bothering you because there is still so much work to do. But you're not doing yourself a favor! Then you can neither enjoy the break, nor get the maximum energy out of it. You're actually wasting valuable time. My tip: accept taking your breaks, no matter how long they are, and most important of all, enjoy them consciously and savor them to the full. This also has to do with mindfulness, which means being able to let go in the respective situation and to consider it consciously and presently, without directing your gaze to the past or future.

Every now and then, take up the guitar for two to three minutes and make time for mini-practices—things are going better again already.
Anke

Eating helps if I'm under stress.
Silvia

Cake!
Tanna

I like the way you think, Tanna.
Silvia

Riding a bike in the evening sunlight, lying in the meadow, and looking at the sky, that's the most calming thing of all! I try to eat better and calm my nerves down by meditation (if I'm fine, I'll let things slide again with meditation . . .) and also brief meditation while I'm working: pause, find a peaceful point, and take several conscious breaths (to solve the problem of shallow breathing due to stress). And meet up with a dear friend; then this immediately blows the stress away!
Carola

Have a cup of tea, outside if possible, look around at what is there, which means observe the sky, plants, animals for a few minutes and notice how the air smells and how the tea tastes. When it's pouring—like now—you can, of course, do this from inside: watch the rain, how the trees are swaying, and of course, the tea still tastes good.
Sybille

I stop the world.
Peter

I try to force myself to do everyday actions in slow motion. Besides this, I avoid parallel "sound reinforcement," such as no music while I am working, not doing several things at the same time, not talking on the phone/working at the same time.
Hannah

Tell me how.
Roberta

I stand back from things. If I'm angry, then I put on running shoes and jog a few laps. Simply going for a walk also helps for thinking things over. The best way to distract myself from everyday stress and get down to work is to spend a lot of time playing computer games. Or I spend time with my wife.
Sven

Go swimming. Diving. Be really kaput afterwards; listen to meditation on YouTube when on the bus. Three liters of "Clear Mind" or "Calming" yogi tea and then classical music. Realizing that it's just a moment; that life is short and that probably the results will be exactly the same thing without extreme stress.
Skadi

Overcome Obstacles

Diagnosis:

Headwind, (Unforeseen) Difficulties

№11

Medical History:

I divide hurdles and obstacles into two categories: your inner hurdles (which are based within yourself) and the outer hurdles (which are placed in your way from outside and possibly by others, on which you have no influence).

Classic hurdles are: (1) resistance to change (here the mere change itself is perceived as a threat); (2) lack of passion and listlessness; (3) financial reasons (budget, lack of money); (4) personal disorientation (such as due to incorrect/not well-defined goals); (5) lack of support from others, denial, perhaps even (obstruction) from others due to conformity, envy, criticism, cynicism; (6) strokes of fate and unforeseen events; (7) inexperience; (8) failure/making mistakes.

The first thing to review is what kind of obstacle is blocking you. Only you can recognize internal hurdles and put them aside (such as by getting rid of prejudices, disorientation, worries, and fears). If you can't do it alone, someone can support you in the process and help you.

If there are external hurdles, you first analyze the situation, and then work out a plan of action and see it through. If it's a financial problem, you should, for example, talk to the client or the target group again. If you're actively hindered in your creative work by others, ask yourself why this is happening and try to convince the "hinderers" about what you want to do and about yourself! One thing you can do is to show them its advantages for their own life (people are egoists, and they see everything in relation to their own living situations). Try to think from their point of view and then act in a more empathetic way. "Hinderers" are also less skeptical and pessimistic regarding a situation or cause to which they have contributed. Therefore, having a say is a possible key here. Anyone who is afraid of change may, in fact, do better by accepting it in small doses. It's also conceivable to try a change on a trial basis, to convince the "hinderers." If that doesn't work, but you still want to stick to your goal, you have to look for other partners or do the work alone and use this headwind as a positive energy boost for yourself.

It's easier to deal with hurdles if you think ahead, because you're more likely to see them coming. If necessary, reckon on the worst (or at least the unforeseen), such as in terms of criticism from others. What could the other side's arguments be? In this way, you might possibly find solutions in advance and cancel out the criticism.

Murphy's Law:

Anything that can go wrong, will go wrong.

Beyond this,
- *Nothing is as simple as it looks.*
- *Everything takes longer than you think it will.*
- *Every solution brings new problems along with it.*
- *Nothing is foolproof; fools are inventive.*
- *You cannot calculate the unpredictable.*

The Inner Hurdle:

Sequence and how to overcome them.

1. *That won't work. I won't waste my time on that.*
2. *It might work, but it's not worth the effort.*
3. *I've already always said it's a good idea.*

Type of First Aid and Prescribed Treatment:

+ ***Apply the "yes, and ..." technique.*** This encouraging corporate coaching method involves not immediately rejecting an unforeseen, initially negative situation, but rather conceiving of it as an opportunity and a stimulus. Take it on with a "yes," then ask about and think about it further with an "and." The aim is that you don't give up, but rather to come to terms with and adjust yourself to the new situation. At the same time, you reflect on your strengths and learn to make better use of them. If you use this technique at least once a day, you will act in a more open and agile way and be more capable of taking criticism in comparable situations in the future.

+ ***Review your expectations & avoid the justice trap.*** Are you expecting too much from yourself and others too soon? Or perhaps you gave up too quickly? Both are due to impatience. (I know what I'm talking about!) Impatience is an internal hurdle that can only be overcome with patience.

Do you possibly expect compensatory justice? Then you have fallen into the justice trap. This is what happens when you assume that life (or other people) owe(s) you something. That harbors a high level of potential for disappointment and frustration. Life just isn't fair sometimes (and doesn't owe you anything).

+ ***Review your goals & avoid the activity trap.*** Sometimes you get in your own way because your goals aren't realistically set, aren't defined clearly enough, or aren't compatible with each other. Review things from time to time to see if they are up to date. Are the contents the same as at the beginning? Is that what I want to achieve? Do I really want that, or are these not my goals (anymore)? Do I do enough on a regular basis to achieve my goals? The danger is that you will lose sight of your goals due to the reasons listed above and fall into the activity trap. That means that all the time you are supposedly occupied with achieving your goal, you are permanently active but aren't making any progress.

Prescribed Treatment

A Restart

Diagnosis:

Lack of input, lack of ideas.

Medical History:

Imagine a computer that has crashed or is only running in a faulty way. This is similar to your situation when you get stuck fast by your blocks. In this situation, you would turn your computer off and then turn it on again, or reset the system by restarting it and then booting it up again. After that, everything usually works again.

Sometimes your thoughts and actions related to your creative work have to be restarted just like a computer. Depending on the situation, you have to decide for yourself which method works best. Should you turn the system off completely for a while, do you restart it, or is the situation so bad that you call in an outside professional for a full system check?

Approach Nº. 1: Shutting down the system means taking a break. Here you can try out the "do-nothing" practice exercise *(see the following box)*. Approach Nº. 2: You do a restart; that is, you forget about what you have done already, and start over (such as from a different perspective). When you do this, the "reframing" and "creative amnesia" practice exercises can help you; *see the following box* for both. Approach Nº. 3: You are blocking in a way so complex that you can't work the problem out by yourself alone.

Type of First Aid and Prescribed Treatment:

✛   *Stimulus word presentation for restarting when you are blocked.* In a group or on your own, pick an arbitrary term (such as by using the "stimulus word technique"; see page 46) and give a spontaneous, three-minute impromptu presentation about it. It's important that the theme has nothing to do with the one that is causing you to block. You are training your spontaneity and imagination with this practice exercise, by steering your creative talents and your thinking in a different direction for a short time. Afterwards, you go back to your actual task, as you would do for a reload/reset.

✛   *The "do-nothing" practice exercise.* Sit down and do nothing, really absolutely nothing! You are not allowed to read, watch TV, play games on your cell phone, make phone calls or surf the internet; nothing at all. Try to endure this situation until you reach your physical limits and/or become totally calm. (The calmness comes after the jitters!) Take enough time for this (thirty minutes is okay, and ninety minutes is a manageable challenge). Try to also turn off your thinking. If you have to think, take note of your thoughts. What do you notice? After this, it will then be easier for you to start over and get back to doing your tasks. The next few times you may only have to think about "sitting it out," and (after a short period of reflection) you will be able to start over right away.

+ *The "reframing" practice exercise.* The term "reframing" comes from psychology and means something like "reinterpretation." The point is (similar to the "yes, and . . ." technique, see page 139) to accept a situation that cannot be changed, in that you reassess the situation from a different point of view and thus learn to see it as a positive opportunity. As an example: you just can't think of a topic for a new blog entry today, so then you write about exactly that! That perhaps might be more interesting than you think.

+ *The "creative amnesia" practice exercise.* As a creative person, you are an insider and an expert in what you do. But if you become involved in an intensive debate, this may lead to "operational blindness." For this reason, you might forget about things that you already know or think you know. But how does it work? For example, you can put aside what you have already created and any work that is half finished, and "forget" about it. Keep working on something else. This creates a kind of artistic-creative amnesia. You forget what something looked like exactly, how you felt about it, and so forth. If you then take up this work again after a while (a few hours, days, weeks), you might no longer be able to imagine that you actually were doing this work or how you did it (at least, that's one effect I see in myself). This effect makes it possible for you to look at your work from the outside with a bit of distance, and to judge it differently—perhaps in a better way because it's more neutral. With a little distance, you can now continue to work, discard it, correct it or complete it.

+ *Brainstorming, mind map, Walt Disney method & the Osborn checklist.* When you restart something, the classic creativity techniques also work very well. You can brainstorm about ideas to resolve your block. You can also depict it in the form of a mind map. You can also analyze your block in the mind map and break down your thought processes. Or you can use the "Walt Disney Method" *(see page 62)* to look at your block and incorporate the three thought perspectives: (1) dreamer, (2) realist, (3) critic.

The "Osborn checklist" can also help for doing a restart, such as for changing and modifying your idea by: (1) using it in a different way, (2) adapting it, (3) changing it, (4) expanding it, (5) minimizing it, (6) replacing it, (7) repositioning it, (8) reversing it, (9) combining it, (10) transforming it.

Appreciate Your Worth

№13

Diagnosis:

Lack of self-esteem

Medical History:

I'm sure that, if you are being encouraged, motivated, and praised by others, it enhances your creative achievement. You have more confidence in yourself, and due to the support and encouragement, you believe more in yourself and in what you are doing. Just as important as being praised by others is to praise and to motivate yourself and to believe firmly in yourself and your abilities. Don't make yourself "small." In this way, you also prevent blocking that might occur due to such things as a lack of self-confidence and a lack of self-esteem.

And to consider yourself to be creative is a great way to become creative! Instead of the word "creative," you can use any adjective here (such as not creative, successful, unsuccessful, professional, unprofessional, rich, poor). This is called auto suggestive thinking. It can help you prevent blocking and help you pursue your goals in a focused manner. One successful role model for autosuggestion is boxing legend **Muhammad Ali**. One of his most famous quotes sums it up: "If my mind can conceive it, and my heart can believe it, then I can achieve it."

Do not let critical voices (internal or external) unsettle you. No one can know beforehand what all is possible! Therefore, essentially no one can judge you in advance (not even yourself). If you have a good feeling about something and are up for trying it out, don't let anyone stop you. Just go ahead and do it with all your passion.

Looking back can also motivate you and increase your self-esteem. Most of the time you just look ahead (and that's a good thing), feel rushed by things, and then get desperate because you have not yet achieved this or that goal. Taking a look back can make it clear to you how successful you have already been and how proud you can be of what you have already achieved. Enjoy it! Stop for a moment and be happy about this. Besides, this moment will give you strength to carry on and motivate you even more not to let the low blows get you down.

The past is one thing, but what makes up most of "life" is the moment, the present (because the past has happened and the future is not yet here). Tip: enjoy the "here and now," the little successes, and appreciate what you are doing.

> # BE PATIENT WITH EVERYTHING, BUT ESPECIALLY WITH YOURSELF.
>
> FRANZ VON SALES

THE WINNER

Type of First Aid and Prescribed Treatment:

+ ***Protective mechanisms can sometimes make you block.*** When you describe yourself as "untalented" or "uncreative," this is probably just a psychological protective mechanism. You are afraid of being judged or condemned for what you are doing.

+ ***Steady growth.*** Start your creative activity by doing small projects; when you become more confident, the projects can become larger and more complex and can grow. Let things grow slowly; your self conception of your creative capabilities will also grow along with your experience—and the risk of being disappointed and blocking is also lower with slow but steady growth

+ ***Accept yourself as you are.*** You are not the sum of your successes or your failures. You're fine the way you are. Nobody is perfect (see page 122). You achieve your inner balance above all through unconditional self-acceptance.

Classify Criticism Objectively

№14

Diagnosis:

Mindfuck, killer phrases, criticism.

Medical History:

Everyone is afraid of criticism. We all want to be liked and praised for what we are (and who we are) and for what we accomplish and create.

There is constructive criticism that will help you progress and that enables you to learn something and improve yourself and your creative work. Constructive criticism can be tough at first; perhaps you can't accept it at first because your self-doubt is too great or your self-confidence is still too limited. But constructive criticism represents some- thing good. It's something you should listen to and look at carefully when you encounter it and deal with it objectively.

Then there is destructive criticism, which demotivates you, robs you of any creative potential and rages at you in a more or less destructive way. It doesn't help you get on in any way. You should avoid it as soon as you encounter it.

Sometimes people criticize because it's easier for them (this may have something to do with laziness or envy). You should always keep in mind that It's easier to criticize yourself or others than to get something up and running and to act. It's a lot easier to be passive. It's much easier to comfortably sit back and regret lost opportunities than to seize on new ones. It's easier to watch and let time go by, than it is to develop ideas and get things moving at the same time! But in this case, the easy way is not the better way, just the more convenient one.

Scientists at **Harvard University** have investigated whether an interpersonal conversation that is perceived as unpleasant and is associated with a feeling of frustration leads to an increase in people's creativity. In a simulated job interview with two different groups, they found that people who are criticized will perform better later than the people who were not criticized. The group of deliberately frustrated test subjects used the resulting frustration to release additional energy and transform it into artistic and creative results. The scientists' theses stated that the criticism could have resulted in the test subjects working even harder on themselves, so they compensated for the weak feedback or criticism with positive results afterwards. Or it had made them think things through even more intensively and delve more into themselves (self-reflection), which spurred their creative work all the more. The assumption is that situations that are annoying and frustrating and drag you down are often more of a creative catalyst.

> Envy is the most honest
> form of flattery.
>
> Wilkie Collins

These are classic killer phrases:
- *I can't think of anything.*
- *You can't do that! It won't amount to anything!*
- *It's all already been tried. We already have that (something better).*
- *That won't work, because . . .*
- *That's unbelievable, because . . .*
- *It's too hard for me.*
- *You aren't allowed to do that.*
- *No one is interested.*
- *Who is going to pay for that?*
- *I don't trust myself to do that.*

Type of First Aid and Prescribed Treatment:

+ *Turn off your inner censor from time to time.* Don't be so hard on yourself. Certainly, self-criticism is good; it can bring you closer to your goals and optimize your work. But self-criticism that is too harsh leads to doubts about one's own actions. This in turn can lead to the situation that you are no longer doing your work, because you have built up too many barriers in your head and are cutting yourself down to size and regulating yourself. Certainly, everyone tries to avoid mistakes in their own work. At the same time, mistakes are not always a bad thing. By making them, we learn and become better.

+ *Question the criticism objectively.* If you are being criticized by others or you are self-critical, ask yourself this: Where does the criticism come from or how did it come about? Is it justified and well-founded? Or does it seem unjust and destructive to you? Does the criticism help you or does it paralyze you? Keep your sense of proportion and your humor; try not to generalize it, not to overestimate it, and not to turn it into a catastrophe (danger of a self-fulfilling prophecy); and take some distance to look at the criticism from an external perspective.

Stop! Pull the Emergency Brake

Diagnosis:

. . . when everything becomes too much.

Medical History:

Sometimes it isn't possible to resolve your blocking so easily with "first aid." If so, it's important to take a good close look at yourself and take the blocking very seriously. If the psychological strain becomes too great and you absolutely don't feel well anymore. or if you are tormenting yourself and are displaying physical symptoms (for example, your immune system becomes weakened or you get sick), then you should definitely pull the emergency brake and say "stop."

Sometimes the obstacles are too high, the goals you have set are too far distant and too unrealistic, the demand for perfection is too great, the criticism is too crushing, and your willpower is too limited or has been exaggerated too much. Often, the problem lies in self-exploitation and excessive demands. In any case, the extent of the creative effort needed, or its proportionality to attaining the result, is no longer in tune with reality, and your body reacts with symptoms of physical and psychological breakdown. These can include physical weakness, a nervous breakdown, burnout—you shouldn't risk any of this in the first place!

Preventive measures are important. Take care of yourself, take note of the first signs of excessive demands or self-exploitation, and do something about it. Take a break more often, say "no" more often, make sure you eat and drink regularly, get enough sleep, don't take criticism so much to heart, don't let yourself become upset, and stay in your own rhythm.

When it's too late for preventive measures and when it all becomes too much, then get professional help. Talk to others about it and get advice. Go to your doctor and consider getting psychotherapeutic support if necessary. Your family doctor can also help you by talking to you, referring you to specialists, and prescribing sick leave.

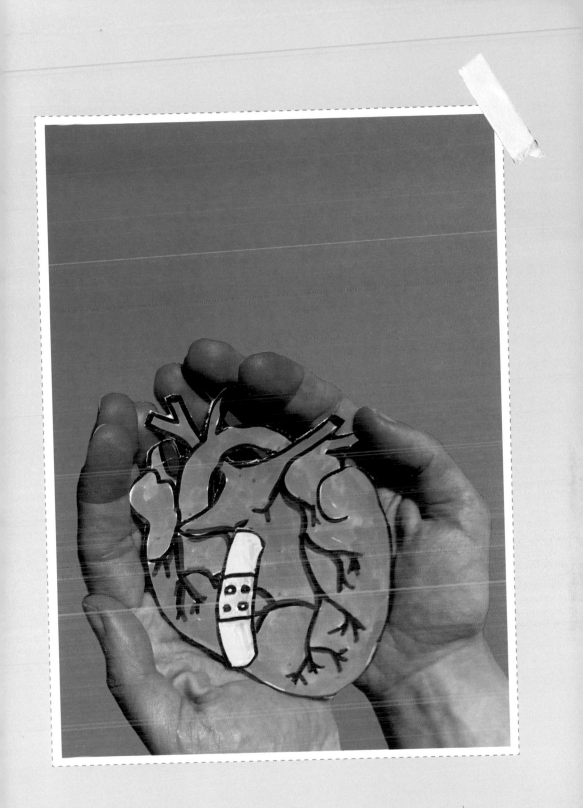

Appendix

Thanks!

Some really wonderful people (once again) supported me in writing this book. I want to say thank you for that!

I am pleased that the many examples that I received from creative people, when requested, made it possible to portray the diversity and breadth of the theme. And therefore, my thanks go to: *Aitch, Jan Augsberg, bildundtonfabrik, Kaja Brandenburger, Café Riptide, Marie Dann, Gerald Dissen, Felix Goltermann, Michel Gondry, Helen Green, Juli Gudehus, Franziska Günther, Christiane Haas, Thomas Hackenberg, Jan von Holleben, HuskMitNavn, Jens Isensee, Jetzt und Hier, Hella Jongerius, Yvonne Kardel, Saskia Kiefert, Sebastian Knecht, Wilhelm Koch, Bernd Labetzsch, Ann-Kathrin Lumpe, Christine Mayer, Katrin Merle, Anja Millen, Ulrike Möltgen, Laura Nagel, Rüdiger und Annette Nehberg, Anna Niestroj, Fabian Nilius, Katharina Preußer, Mandy Röhr, Helmut Smits, Lisa Tegtmeier, Sebastian Thies, VOR Werbeagentur,* and *Wessinger und Peng,* as well as *Lisa Wohlsen.*

My personal thanks go to my intern *Nina Sieverding.*

A big thank-you goes to *Juliane Wenzl, Hannah Robold,* and *Anne Kliche,* who (not only, but also) made themselves available as my guinea pigs for the "creative types"

> "Joy is the simplest form of gratitude."
>
> Karl Barth

test. Many thanks for their regular participation on Facebook to *Petrus Akkordeon, Apfelhase, Sybille Benedict-Lux, Kristina Brasseler, Ralph Bergel, Felix Bork, Arinda Craciun, Johannes Esser, Anke Faust, Sven Geske, Peter M. Glantz, Ulrike Heidemann, Doro Herrmann, Eva Jaeger-Nilius, Kathrin Jebsen, Silvia Karkut, Christin Kloss, Daria Komleva Litvinova, Tanja Krach, Ariane Krahl, Gila von Meissner, Marie Christine Müller, Tessa Rath, Saramin, Hannah Schrage, Anita Schwörer, Carola Sturm, Skadi Sturm, Meike Töpperwien, Charlotte Wagner,* and *Bille Weidenbach.* Another thank-you goes to my wonderful *Facebook group, Kreativrezepte [Creative Prescriptions],* (facebook.com/groups/kreativrezepte), whom I consulted for advice every now and then.

And my heartfelt thanks to my publisher. That means thanks to *Matthias, Adela,* and *Patrizia Haupt,* who are so open and warm to me; to *Regine Balmer* for her overview and perspective; to my editor *Heidi Müller,* who has enthusiastically supported and further developed the book project; to *Gabi Bortot* for the image research; to *Daniela Vacas* for the help in production; to *Claudia Huboi* for proofreading, and to *Martina Räber* for marketing!

Special thanks go to my *parents, Timo* and *Bernadette,* and to the four ladies at *Tatendrang* (Thirst for Action) for listening and being there for me.

Recommended Reading

Bergmann, Roberta, *Die Grundlagen des Gestaltens* [*The Fundamentals of Design*], second edition, Haupt Verlag, Bern, Switzerland, 2017.

Berzbach, Frank, *Die Kunst, ein kreatives Leben zu führen: Oder Anregung zu Achtsamkeit* [*The Art of Leading a Creative Life: Or Stimulating Mindfulness*], seventh edition, Verlag Hermann Schmidt, Mainz, Germany, 2015.

Bock, Petra, *Mindfuck — Warum wir uns selbst sabotieren und was wir dagegen tun konnen* [*Mindfuck — Why We Sabotage Ourselves and What We Can Do about It*], Knaur Verlag, Munich, 2011.

Curry, Mason, *Daily Rituals: How Artists Work* [German version: *Musenküsse— Die täglichen Rituale berühmter Künstler*], third edition, Kein & Aber AG Zurich— Berlin, 2014.

Kelly, David, and Tom Kelly, *Creative Confidence: Unleashing the Creative Potential with- in Us All* [German version: *Kreativität und Selbstvertrauen — Der Schlüssel zu Ihrem Kreativbewusstsein*], second edition, Verlag Hermann Schmidt, Mainz, Germany, 2014.

Lehrer, Jonah, *Imagine! - Wie das kreative Gehirn funktioniert* [*How the Creative Brain Works*] C.H.Beck, Munich, 2014.

Lord, James, *A Giacometti Portrait* [German version: *Alberto Giacometti — Ein Portrait*], Ullstein Taschen buchverlag, Munich, 2001.

Nehberg, Rüdiger, *Die Autobiographie* [*Autobiography*], Piper Verlag GmbH, Munich, 2005.

Sylvester, David, *Interviews with Francis Bacon* [German version: *Gespräche mit Francis Bacon*], seventh edition: expanded new edition, Prestel, Munich, 1997.

Sources

P. 8   Matisse quote from: Will Gompertz, *Denken wie ein Künstler* [*Think like an Artist*], Dumont Buchverlag, Cologne, 2016, p. 168.

P. 8   Definition cf. https://de.wikipedia.org/wiki/Do_it_yourself, status as of: 01/03/2017.

P. 9   Steinbeck quote from: same as source for p. 8: Will Gompertz publication, p. 53.

P. 10   Definition cf. https://de.wikipedia.org/wiki/Kreativität, status as of: 01/03/2017.

P. 10   Gompertz quote from: same as source for p. 8: Will Gompertz publication, p. 63.

P. 10   cf. Robert W. Weisberg, *Creativity: Beyond the Myth of Genius* [German version: *Kreativität und Begabung: Was wir mit Mozart, Einstein und Picasso gemeinsam haben*], Spektrum der Wissenschaft, Heidelberg, 1989.

P. 11   cf. Table: Manuela Pohl, *Kreative Kompetenz* [*Creative Competence*], Cornelsen Verlag, Berlin, 2012, p. 28.

P. 11   cf. Dr. Matthias Nöllke, *Kreativitätstechniken* [*Techniques for Creativity*], seventh edition, Haufe-Lexware GmbH & Co KG, Freiburg, Germany, 2015, p. 12 ff.

P. 12   cf. Mihály Csikszentmihályi, *Kreativität* [*Creativity*], Klett-Cotta, Stuttgart, Germany, 2010.

P. 12   Wood quote from: Daniel Goleman, Paul Kaufman, and Michael Ray, *The Creative Spirit* [German version: *Kreativität entdecken*], third edition, Deutscher Taschenbuch Verlag GmbH & Co. KG, Munich, 2003, p. 22.

P. 13   cf. https://de.wikipedia.org/wiki/Ingrid_Noll, status as of 01/09/2017.

P. 33   cf. Ryder Carroll website: http://bulletjournal.com, status as of 02/10/2017.

P. 46   Study on creative chaos, information at: http://www.apa.org/monitor/2013/10/messy-desk.aspx; Quadbeck-Seeger quote from: https://www.aphorismen.de/zitat/83412, status as of 2/24/2017.

P. 66   cf. http://teamrock.com/feature/2014-05-28/david-bowie-on-songwriting.

P. 75   cf. https://www.dezeen.com/2009/02/06/pelle-mikkel-and-gullspira-by-hella-jongerius-for-ikea.

P. 78   Giacometti quotes cf. James Lord, *Alberto Giacometti – Ein Portrait*, Ullstein Taschenbuchverlag, Munich, 2001.

P. 84   Nietzsche quote from http://www.gutzitiert.de/zitat_autor_friedrich_wilhelm_nietzsche_1033.html, status as of: 04/28/2017.

P. 92   Wooden stick task developed and taught in collaboration with Prof. Alexandra Martini.

P. 94   Quote from http://www.3sat.de/page/?source=/scobel/169982/index.html, status as of 05/13/2017.

P. 95   Quote from http://karrierebibel.de/selektiven-wahrendung-beispiel-test/, status as of:05/13/2017.

P. 98   cf. http://www.gateway-online.de/de/beruf-karriere-3-but/role-models/153-was-sind-role-models, status as of 05/19/2017.

P. 98   Ernst quote from: http://www.gutzitiert.de/zitat_autor_otto_ernst_364.html, status as of 05/19/2017.

P. 104   cf. http://www.wissenschaft.de/leben-umwelt/psychologie/-/journal_content/56/12054/3450619/Kreativer-durch-Bewegungs/, status as of 06/19/2017.

P. 114   Assa quote from: https://www.aphorismen.de/zitat/126908, status as of 04/13/2017.

P. 123   Sutton, Rodriguez quote: IDEO, d.school Stanford from: David and Tom Kelley, *Kreativität und Selbstvertrauen*, Verlag Hermann Schmidt, second edition, Mainz, Germany, 2014, p. 64.

P. 123   Flink quote IDEO, from David und Tom Kelley, *Kreativität und Selbstvertrauen*, Verlag Hermann Schmidt, second edition, Mainz, Germany, 2014, p. 65.

P. 124   Allen story, cf. Mason Currrey, *Musenküsse – Die täglichen Rituale berühmter Künstler*, Kein & Aber AG, third edition, Zurich–Berlin, 2014, p. 121 ff.

P. 127   Selacher quote from https://www.aphorismen.de/zitat/76895, status as of 07/11/2017.

P. 129 Watson quote from Alexander Jeanmaire: *Der kreative Funke. Handbuch für Kreativität und Lebenskunst* [*The Creative Spark. Handbook for Creativity and the Art of Living*], ars momentum Kunstverlag GmbH, Witten, Germany, 2006, p. 133.

P. 133 Quote above, cf. https://de.wikipedia.org/wiki/Weniger_ist_mehr, status as of 07/12/2017.

P. 135 DMN, cf. https://de.wikipedia.org/wiki/Default_Mode_Network, status as of 07/12/2017.

P. 136 Quotes from https://www.facebook.com/groups/kreativrezepte; with kind approval of the group members, quotes from: Sabine Benedict-Lux, Roberta Bergmann, Anke Faust, Sven Geske, Peter M. Glantz, Tanja Lärm, Hannah Robold, Silvia, Carola Sturm, and Skadi Sturm, quotes slightly changed orthographically, status as of 11/14/2017.

P. 137 same as source for p. 136.

P. 139 Box "The Inner Hurdle," cf. Michael LeBoeuf, *Imagination Inspiration Innovation Kreative Kräfte nutzen* [*Use Creative Power*], mvg verlag—Moderne Verlagsgesellschaft mbH, second edition, Munich, 1991.

P. 141 On Havard University cf. http://karrierebibel.de/kreativer-haben/, status as of 07/02/2017.

P. 142 Ali quote from: http://www.rp-online.de/sport/boxen/muhammad-ali-seine-besten-zitate-und-sprueche-bid-1.2672221, status as of 07/14/2017.

P. 143 Sales quote from: https://www.aphorismen.de/zitat/13000, status as of 07/14/2017.

P. 145 Collins quote from: http://www.quotez.net/german/wilkie_collins.htm, status as of 07/14/2017.

P. 150 Barth quote from: http://zitate.net/karl-barth-zitate, status as of 07/15/2017.

Photos and Illustrations

Pages 2, 5, 14-15, 21, 22-23, 24, 28-29, 31, 34, 38, 48, 69-71, 92, 98, 110-111, 125, 127, 143, 147-149 © Roberta Bergmann

Pages 25, 27
© Anna Niestroj, Blinkblink

Page 30
© Michel Gondry, www.usinedefilmsamateurs.com

Pages 32-33
BulletJournal: © Ann-Kathrin Lumpe, photos: © Roberta Bergmann

Pages 35-37, 46-47, 77, 93, 112-113
© Nina Sieverding, www.ninasieverding.com.

Page 39
© Juli Gudehus, www.juligudehus.net

Pages 40-41
© Lisa Tegtmeier, www.lisategtmeier.de

Pages 42-43
Shutterstock/Dragon Images

Page 43
Photo: *White Washing Parade,* © Regine Nahrwold, www.freigeistreich.de, www.jensisensee.de

Page 44
MoMa umbrella © Tibor Kalman (designer)

Pages 44-45
Erwin Wurm, *Spruce,* © 2017, ProLitteris, Zurich, photo © Roberta Bergmann

Page 45
© Rüdiger Nehberg, TARGET e.V.
The association TARGET e.V. is committed to stopping the crime of *female genital mutilation.* You can support this work as a sponsor. Information at: www.target-nehberg.de.

Page 66

David Bowie portrait: © Helen Green, www.
helengreenillustration.com; Snippet technique
photo: © Roberta Bergmann.

Page 67

Top: © Katrin Merle, www.katrinmerle.de
Bottom: © HuskMitNavn, www.huskmitnavn.dk

Page 73

Top: © Juliane Wenzl, www.ingestalt.de
Bottom: Wikimedia Commons, Utagawa
Kuniyoshi (PD)

Page 75

Top, book cover: © Tonia Wiatrowski, Inga Marie
Ramcke, *Reiseführer für Tiere* [*Travel Guidebook
for Animals*], Folio Verlag, Bolzano/Vienna, 2015;
Author portrait by Tonia Wiatrowski and Inga
Marie Ramcke: © Annette Schrader
Center left: "PS Pelle" © IKEA
Center right: "Gullspira" © Gerrit Schreurs, IKEA
Bottom left: "Design Process IKEA Roots Pelle" ©
Jongeriuslab,
Bottom right: "Process IKEA Roots" © IKEA

Page 78

Photo of Alberto Giacometti: photograph by
Ernst Scheidegger © 2017, Ernst Scheidegger
Archive Foundation, Zurich

Page 79

Top, photos: © Wilhelm Koch
Bottom: © Michel Gondry, "1000 Portraits"

Page 81

Top: Wikimedia Commons, Phrood (PD) Center:
© music theater group "jetztodernie" ["Now or
Never"] of the IGS Franzsches Feld,
Braunschweig, Germany, musical direction: Felix
Goltermann, director: Kaja Brandenburger,

actors, portrait-format photo: Luisa Empacher
(Ilse), Niclas Peter Bahl (Moritz), actors
landscape-format photo: Tetje Groth (Wendla),
Riaan Alexander Schlez (Melchior), photos:
© Roberta Bergmann
Bottom: © Roberta Bergmann, Frank Wedekind,
"Frühlings Erwachen," kunstanstifter verlag,
Mannheim, 2014

Page 83

Top, book cover: © Rod Green, *Monty Python's
Flying Circus. Hidden Treasures. With a foreword
by the Pythons*, English original edition, Edition
Olms, Zurich, 2017
Bottom, book cover: © Christophe Delbrouck,
Frank Zappa & les Mères de l'Invention, Le Castor
Astral, Pantin, France 2017

Page 85

Top: © Roberta Bergmann.
Bottom: © smarticular.net, Sebastian Knecht

Pages 86-87

Top: © Marie Dann, www.mariedann.de
Bottom: © Roberta Bergmann.

Page 89

Top: © Improtheater "Jetzt und Hier,"
Braunschweig, Germany, photo
Top from left to right: Claudia Soluk (Keyboard),
Christiane Hansen-Hildebrand, Silke Köchling,
Heike Nerger, Frank Gebhard, Stefan Kruse;
Bottom, from left to right: Heike Nerger, Frank
Gebhard, Stefan Kruse, Silke Köchling, photos:
© Roberta Bergmann Bottom: © ZDF/btf, the
podcast "Gute Arbeit Impro" is produced by
bildundton-fabrik on behalf of ZDF for funk -
the content network of ARD and ZDF German
public broadcasters.

Index

A

Abramović, Marina 65
Aitch 58
Akkordeon, Petrus 55
Ali, Muhammad 142
Allen, Woody 124
Analogies 108
Anger 114, 126
Apfelhase 55
Art vending machine 110
Assa, Aba 114
Augsberg, Jan 119
Autosuggestion 68 , 142

B

Bacon, Francis 50
Beck, Harry 108
Bergel, Ralph 54
Bergmann, Roberta 5, 53, 55,
    81, 111
Blocking 114
Bock, Petra 122
Bork, Felix 55
Bowie, David 66
Brainstorming 141
Brainwriting 30
Brasseler, Kristina 55
Breaks 56, 70, 104, 134, 146
Brenner, Ulrike 52
Broadway 81
Bucket list 127
Budget 25, 114
Bullet Journal 32
Burnout 146

C

Cage, John 44
Carnegie Hall 78
Carroll, Lewis 61
Carroll, Ryder 33
Catharsis 36, 92
Chance 66

Chance story 80
Chaos 50
Comfort zone (getting out) 118
Creative amnesia practice
    exercise 141
Creativity 10, 28
Creativity killer 125
Creativity prescriptions 28
Creative types 14, 106
Criticism 144
Contact improvisation 88
Collins, Wilkie 145
Craciun, Arinda 55
Cradle-to-cradle 47
Csíkszentmihályi, Mihály 12

D

da Vinci, Leonardo 54
Dalí, Salvador 61, 106
Dann, Marie 87
DaWanda 109
de Bono, Edward 11, 60
Dilts, Robert B. 62
Disney, Walt 62, 141
Dissen, Gerald 101
Distraction traps 27
Do-it-yourself 8
Dream 56, 134
Dream diary 56

E

Elevator pitch 76
Elevator statement 76
Erat, Elke 55
Ernst, Otto 98
Escher, M.C. 106
Esser, Johannes 54
Etching 85
Evernote 46
Experiment 84

F

Fears 30, 114
First aid 112
Flink, Chris 123
Flow 12, 124
Free jazz 88
Free ticket 129
Frühlings Erwachen (Spring
    Awakening) 81
Fuck-up event 123

G

Gardner, Howard, 11
Giacometti, Alberto 78
Giger, H.R. 106
Gimmebar 32
Gompertz, Will 10
Gondry, Michel 30, 79
Gudehus, Juli 39
Guilford, Joy Paul 11
Gute Arbeit Impro 89

H

Haas, Christiane 115
Harvard University 144
Headstand method 44
Heidemann, Ulrike 55
Hermit 64
Herrmann, Doro 55
Herzallgäuerliebst 62
Hoheisel, Timo 58
Horizons, broadening your 86
Humor 97, 102 , 127
HuskMitNavn 67

I

Idea book 34
Idea box 34, 46
Idea poster 34
Ideas, visualizing 96
IKEA 75
Improvising 88

Incubation 12
Interdisciplinary 52, 74, 110
Intuition 34, 36, 92
Isensee, Jens 42

J
Jaeger-Nilius, Eva 55
Jam session 88
Jebsen, Kathrin 55
Jetzt und Hier 89
Jongerius, Hella 75

K
Kalman, Tibor 44
Kardel, Yvonne 109
Karkut, Silvia 55
Kerber, Daniel 101
Kierkegaard 134
Killer phrases 125, 144
Kloss, Christin 55
Koch, Wilhelm 79
Krahl, Ariane 55
Kristiansen, Kjeld Kirk 42
Kuniyoshi, Utagawa 73
kunstanstifter Verlag 81

L
Labetzsch, Bernd 52
Lego Serious Play 42
Less is more 132
Litvinova, Daria 55
Lumpe, Ann-Kathrin 33

M
Materials collection 38
Mathematics 58
Matisse, Henri 8
Mayer, Christine 47
Merle, Katrin 67
Merton, Robert K. 98
Micro-library 110
Milestone method 120, 132

Millen, Anja 57
Mind map 24, 32, 141
Mindfuck 122, 144
Mindfulness 8, 70, 94, 114, 116,
    135, 146
Minimalism 90
Minimal Music 58
Mission statement 36
Möltgen, Ulrike 51
Mona Lisa 54
Monty Python 83
Mood board 32
Motivation, intrinsic 10
Motivational mantra 127
Motivator 131
Müller, Marie 55
Müller, Michaela 58
Murphy's Law(s) 139
Museum of Modern Art 44

N
Nagel, Laura 57
nat-2 101
Nehberg, Rüdiger 44
Network, own 86, 131
Niagara syndrome 128
Niemann, Christoph 48
Nietzsche, Friedrich Wilhelm
    84
Nilius, Fabian 95
No ("say no") 120
Noll, Ingrid 13
Nothing (do-nothing exercise)
    140

O
Obstacles 138
Ogden, Perry 51
Osborn checklist 141

P
Palm, Lionel 101

Panten, Joachim 69
Pareidolia 95
Peer group 72
Perfection 122, 143
Perception, selective 56, 94
Perspective (change) 62
Picasso, Pablo 13
Pinterest 32
Podcast 89
Practice 78, 129
Praise, self 68, 142
Preußer, Katharina 109
Process, the creative 12

Q
Quadbeck-Seeger, Prof. Dr.
    Hans-Jürgen 50
Questionnaire 14, 37, 99

R
Rage 114, 126
Ramcke, Inga Marie 75
Rath, Tessa 55
Recombine 52
Reframing exercise 141
Research spirit 100
Restart 140
Reward principle 68
Rhetoric 77
Riptide 65
Rituals 124
Rodriguez, Diego 123
Role model 98, 142
Room in a Box 101

S
Santa Clara University 104
Saramin 55
Sater, Steven 81
Schiaparelli, Elsa 61
Schrage, Hannah 55
Schweinehund, inner (baser

instincts) 68, 124
Schwörer, Anita 55
Selacher, Alfred 127
Self-praise 68
Serendipity principle 66
Sheik, Duncan 81
Showering 12, 56, 124
Shrigley, David 90
Sieverding, Nina 93
Simple 90
Smarticular.net 85
Smits, Helmut 97
Snippet technique 46
Society6 58
Sparring partner 72, 74, 130
Spring Awakening 81
Stanford University 104
Status quo 24
Steinbeck, John 9
Stimulus word technique 46,
    140
Storytelling 40, 80
Stuck, Franz von 81
Subconscious 56
Support 130
Surrealism 106
Sutton, Prof. Bob 123
Synchronized drawing 125

T
latendrang-Design 53, 111
Teamwork 64
Teytmeier, Lisa 41
Thies, Sebastian 101
Think outside the box 110, 119
Thinking, divergent and lateral
    11, 82
Timetable 26
Timing 26, 120
tinkeringschool 91
To-do list 26, 30, 32
Töpperwien, Meike 55

Trial and error 84
Twitter 90

U
Ulay 65
UNICEF 75
University of Minnesota 50
Upcycling 62, 85, 110

V
van der Rohe, Ludwig Mies
    133
Visions pin board 24, 32
von Holleben, Jan 107
von Meissner, Gila 55
von Sales, Franz 143
VOR advertising agency 102

W
W & H questions 40
Wagner, Charlotte 55
Wall, the fourth 83
Watson, Tom 128
Wedekind, Frank 81
Weidenbach, Bille 55
Weisberg, Robert W. 10
Wenzl, Iuliane 73
Wessinger and Peng 103
Wiatrowski, Tonia 53, 75
Willpower 128
Workplace 25
Wurm, Erwin 44

Y
"Yes-and ." technique 139,
    141
YouTube 109

Z
Zappa, Frank 83

Roberta Bergmann lectures on topics of design principles and making. A freelance artist, illustrator, and book designer, she has been personally involved with the theme of creativity since she was first able to hold a pen. During her more than 15 years as a creative professional, she has been confronted with its challenges on an almost daily basis. Bergmann is the author of several books, including *The Basics of Design*. She lives in Braunschweig, Germany. www.robertabergmann.de.